Cooking Minnesotan
you-betcha!

by
Dr. Duane R. Lund

Recipes from the
Kitchens of Minnesota

Traditional Minnesota Cooking

Ethnic Contributions

Enjoying the Fruits of
Minnesota's Woods and Lakes.

Distributed by
Adventure Publications, Inc.
P.O. Box 269
Cambridge, MN 55008

ISBN 1-885061-94-3

Cooking Minnesotan

First Printing, 2001

Printed in the United States of America
by
Nordell Graphic Communications, Inc.
Staples, Minnesota 56479

INTRODUCTION

Minnesota has been a true melting pot of races and nationalities. Each has contributed its own rich traditions of cooking.

Over the years a fairly unique cuisine has developed that is truly Minnesotan. Although national dishes remain clearly discernible, cooks have taken the best of each to develop their own specialties.

Visitors to Minnesota leave with extraordinary dining experiences among their favorite memories.

This book is divided into three parts:

PART I

Recipes from Minnesota's Lakes and Woodlands.

PART II

Traditional Minnesota Cooking. The kind of recipes found in church cookbooks and at church suppers.

PART III

Ethnic contributions to Minnesota cooking.

TABLE OF CONTENTS

INTRODUCTION

PART 1
Recipes From Minnesota's Woods and Lakes

FISH
Minnesota Baked Northern Pike with Raisin Stuffing /13
Walleye Fillets in Beer Batter /14
Cheese-coated Perch /14
Coated with Cracker Crumbs /15
Fish Patties /15
Panfish with Parsley and Dill /15
Pickled Northern Pike (or other fish) /16
Shore Lunch /16

GAME BIRDS
Half-Ducks on a Bed of Rice /17
Gourmet Roast Duck /18
Duck Gravy /19
Parboiled Ducks or Geese /19
Onion Soup Mix Treatment for Those Tough Old Birds /19
Pheasant in Sour Cream /20
Pheasant or Grouse Breasts with Wild Rice /20
Wild Rice and Grouse Casserole /21

GAME ANIMALS
Big Game Stew /22
Small Game Mulligan /22
Jerky /23

WILD RICE RECIPES
Five Methods of Preparing Wild Rice /24
Wild Rice with Cream of Mushroom Soup /25
Nutty Rice /26
Wild Rice with Mushrooms /26
Wild Rice with Sirloin /27
Creamy Mushroom Wild Rice Soup /28
Wild Rice Bread /28

The Woodlands as our Garden

MUSHROOMS
Morel Mushrooms / *30*
Puff Ball Mushrooms / *30*
Shelf Fungus / *30*
Baked Mushrooms / *31*
Mushroom Stuffing for Fish or Fowl / *31*

WILD FRUITS AND BERRIES
Chokecherry Syrup / *32*
Chokecherry and Wine Jelly / *32*
Blueberry Jelly / *33*
Blueberry Sauce / *33*
Blueberry Muffins / *34*
Wild Cranberries / *34*
Cranberry Relish / *34*
Cranberry Stuffing / *35*
Pincherry Jelly / *35*
Spicy Jams and Jellies / *35*
Mixed Fruit Jellies / *35*
Wild Plum Butter / *36*

PART II
Traditional Minnesota Cooking

MINNESOTA BREAKFASTS
Pancakes from Scratch / *37*
Gourmet Cakes / *38*
Waffles / *38*
French Toast / *38*
Scrambled Eggs / 39
Minnesota Skillet Breakfast #1 / *39*
Minnesota Skillet Breakfast #2 / *40*
Lake of the Woods Omelet / *40*
Blueberry Muffins #2 / *41*

SOUPS
Beer-Cheese Soup / *42*
Baked Potato Soup / *42*
Barley with Beef and Vegetables / *43*
Fresh Garden Tomato Soup / *43*

SALADS
Caramel Apple Salad / *44*
Frog Eyed Salad / *44*

HOT DISHES
Hamburger Hot Dish with Mushrooms / *45*
Hamburger-Tomato Hot Dish / *45*
Wild Rice and Hamburger Hot Dish / *46*
Corned Beef Hot Dish / *46*
Calico Beans Hot Dish / *47*
Hamburger and Noodle Hot Dish with Peas / *47*
Fish and Potato Hot Dish / *48*
Tunafish Hot Dish / *48*
Sweet Potato Hot Dish / *48*
Cheesy Vegetable Hot Dish / *49*
Walleye and Potato Hot Dish / *49*
Pheasant, Partridge or Duck Wild Rice Hot Dish / *50*
Sauerkraut with Meat Hot Dish / **51**
Spam Hot Dish / *51*

TRADITIONAL MEAT RECIPES
Roasts / *52*
All Purpose Gravy Recipe / *52*
Steaks /*53*
   Broiled / *53*
   Baked / *53*
   Mushroom Style / *53*
   Swiss Steak / *53*
   Baked Steak with Onion Soup Mix / *54*
Ham on the Grill with Barbecue Sauce / 54
Baked Chops / *55*

DESSERTS
Chocolate Chip Cookies / *55*
Peanut Butter Cookies / *56*
Sugar Cookies / *56*
Molasses Cookies / *57*
Brownies / *57*
Rhubarb Pie / *58*
Blueberry Pie / *58*
Brown Betty / *59*

Glorified Rice / *59*
Fruitcake / 59
Angel Food Dessert / *60*
Rice Krispie Bars / *60*

PICNIC AND CABIN COOKING
Potato Salad with Dill / *61*
Baked Beans / *61*
Hamburgers / *62*
Hot Dogs (Wieners/Brats) / *62*
Roasting Ears / *62*
Chili / *63*
Stew / *63*

LOGGING CAMP COOKING
Sourdough Pancakes / *64*
Parsnips, Rutabagas and Potato Soup / *64*
Pot Roast / *65*
Baking Powder Biscuits / *65*

PART III
Ethnic Contributions to Minnesota Cooking

SCANDINAVIAN
Swedish Pancakes / *66*
Swedish Meatballs / *66*
Lutefisk / *67*
Potato Lefse / *68*
Fruit Soup / *69*
Finnish Soup (Moijakka) / *69*
Swedish Rye Bread (Limpa) / *70*
Danish Pastries / *71*
Norwegian Crullers / *72*
Veal Roast with Dill Sauce / *72*
Rullepolse (Scandinavian Meat Roll) / *73*
Head Cheese / *73*
The Smorgasbord / *74*
  Sandwich Options / *74*
  Smoked Meats / *74*
  Shrimp / *75*
  Smoked Fish and Cream Cheese / *75*
  Herring and Potatoes / *75*
  Caviar / *75*

Ham / *75*
Cheeses / *75*
Salted Herring / *76*
Full Loaf Sandwich / *76*

GERMAN
Black Rye Bread / *76*
German Potato Salad / *77*
Cabbage Strudel / *77*
Goose with Sausage Dressing / *78*
Goose with Sauerkraut Dressing / *79*
Sauerbraten / *79*

ENGLISH
Beef Tenderloin with Sherry Glaze / *80*
Horseradish Slaw / *81*
Lamb Chops with Mint / *81*
Game Birds in Sherry Cream Sauce / *82*
Fowl Basted with Apple Sauce / *82*
Stuffed Goose (Chestnut and Sausage Stuffing) / *83*

IRISH
Corned Beef and Cabbage / *84*
Stew / *85*
Split Pea Soup / *85*

POLISH
Filled Dumplings (Pierogi) / *86*
Fish Soup (Zupa z Ryby) / *87*
Duck Soup (Czarnina) / *88*

ITALIAN
Party Toasts (Brushetta) / *88*
Fettuccine Alfredo with Mushrooms / *89*
Anchovy Salad / *89*
Seafood Soup / *90*

AFRICAN AMERICAN
Creamy Peanut Soup / *90*
Tabboulah / *91*
Harira (Stew) / *91*
Shrimp and Chicken with Rice / *92*
Stove Top Chicken / *93*

NATIVE AMERICAN
Wild Rice Stew (Ojibwe) / *94*
Pumpkins and Squash (Ojibwe and Dakota Sioux) / 94
Maize (Corn - Dakota Sioux) / *95*
Rabbit or Grey Squirrel (Ojibwe) / *96*
Pickled Tongue (Ojibwe) / *96*
Heart (Ojibwe) / *97*
Poached Whitefish (Ojibwe) / *97*

CZECHOSLOVAKIAN
Kolaches / *98*

JEWISH
Potato Latkes #1 / **99**
Potato Latkes #2 (With Apples) / *99*
Matzo Balls (Served in Soups) / *100*

WELSH
Rarebit / *100*
Potato Soup / *101*

Contributions of More Recent Minnesotans

HISPANIC
Salsa / *101*
Guacamole / *102*
Tamales / *102*
Chicken Chili over Rice / *103*
Stuffed Bell Peppers / *104*
Egg Timbales / *105*

ASIAN
Rice Cakes / *105*
Fried Rice / *106*
Eggplant with Pork / *106*
Chicken with Egg Crust Shrimp / *107*
Spicy Shrimp with Tomato Sauce / *107*
Poached Duck / *108*
Sweet and Sour Pork / *108*
Fish and Eggs / *109*
Sweet Rice Pudding / *109*

INDIAN

Roast Leg of Lamb / *110*
Lentils and Curried Rice / *111*
Curried Vegetables / *111*
Curried Paste for Seasoning / *112*

Part I

RECIPES FROM MINNESOTA'S LAKES AND WOODLANDS

American Indians who lived in this area we now call Minnesota depended almost entirely on nature for their food - and they knew how to prepare and enjoy it. Early European immigrants quickly learned from the Ojibwe and the Dakota Sioux that the lakes, streams, woodlands and prairies were at least as important sources of nutrition as their own farms and gardens.

Today, Minnesotans still harvest fish, game, mushrooms, berries, wild rice and more to augment their diet. They know that these foods are both healthy and tasty. To enjoy these extraordinary treats is a privilege denied in most states.

Fish

Minnesota Baked Northern Pike with Raisin Stuffing

This recipe also works well with other large fish. On the other hand, all fish are not good baked; even the tasty walleye or the flavorful bass are only fair unless they receive special treatment and seasonings.
Northerns should weigh four pounds or more, whitefish, walleyes and bass, at least three.

Preparing the fish: Scale and gut the fish; remove the head, tail and all fins. Wash and dry the fish, inside and out.
Score the back of the fish with cross-section cuts about three inches apart–down to the backbone.
Salt and pepper, inside and out and in the cuts.

Preparing the stuffing:
1 cup raisins
1/4 lb. butter (added to one cup hot water)
2 cups croutons or dry bread crumbs
1 large onion, chopped but not too fine
salt and pepper
1 cup chopped bologna (or wieners or polish sausage or luncheon meat or breakfast meat)

Place the croutons, raisins, meat and onions in a bowl. Salt and pepper lightly while stirring the ingredients together.

Add and stir in the butter-hot water mixture just before stuffing the fish.

Lay a sheet of foil on the bottom of the roaster.

Stuff the fish (loosely) and place upright on the sheet of foil.

Fold the foil up along both sides of the fish–do not cover the back. The foil will hold in the stuffing. If your fish is too long for the roaster, you may cut it in two and bake the two sections side by side.

Leftover stuffing or additional stuffing may be baked in a foil package alongside the fish or even outside the roaster.

Place a strip of bacon and a slice of onion, alternately, over each score (or cut).

Cover the roaster and place in a pre-heated, 300° oven. After one hour, remove cover and continue to bake until the meat becomes flaky and separates from the backbone (as viewed from the end of the fish). This should take about another half-hour, depending on the size of the fish.

Transfer the baked fish to a platter. Cut through the backbone at each score mark, separating the fish into serving-size portions. The stuffing may be lifted out with each portion as it is served.

Serve with tartar sauce and/or lemon.

Walleye Fillets in Beer Batter

Pour one-half cup of beer into a bowl and let stand overnight or until "flat".

Add the beer and a tbsp. of cooking oil to two cups of white flour. Mix. Beat the whites of three eggs until stiff and work them into the batter. If mixture is too heavy, add a little water.

Dip the fillets into the batter and deep fry in very hot cooking oil until golden brown. The batter tends to insulate the fish so make certain they are done before serving.

Cheese-Coated Perch

Save those larger perch and give them this treatment:
1 pound fresh perch fillets (or other freshwater fish)
1/4 cup all purpose flour
1 beaten egg
1 tsp. salt
dash pepper
1/4 cup fine dry bread crumbs
1/4 cup grated Parmesan cheese
1/4 cup shortening
1 eight ounce can tomato sauce
1/2 tsp. sugar
1/2 tsp. dried basil leaves, crushed

Cut fish into serving size portions. Coat with flour and dip into a mixture of egg, salt and pepper, then dip into a mixture of bread crumbs and cheese. Fry fish slowly in a skillet or hot shortening until browned on one side. Turn and brown other side. Combine tomato sauce, 1/4 cup water, sugar and basil in a saucepan. Simmer 10 minutes and serve with the fish.

Coated with Cracker Crumbs

The simplest recipe for fried fillets and maybe the best:

Using a rolling pin, crush salted crackers into fine crumbs. Stir in a generous portion of lemon pepper. Prepare an egg wash by beating an egg (more if you are frying a lot of fish) into 2 cups of water.

Dip the fillets into the egg wash, then into the cracker crumbs and fry in a well oiled hot skillet, browning both sides.

Fish Patties

Chop two cups of flaked, boneless fish-either raw or cooked fish may be used. Almost any kind of fish works just fine. This is a very good way to use-up leftovers. Combine the chopped fish with:

1 egg

1/2 cup chopped onion

pinch or two of salt

1 tsp. lemon pepper

1/2 cup chopped green pepper

Add water to 1 cup "complete" pancake mix until it has the consistency you would use to make pancakes. Add the batter to the fish and other ingredients until it has the consistency (looks like) potato salad.

Drop large spoonfuls on a hot, greased grill or large, non-stick frying pan, forming patties. Fry until well-browned on both sides.

Serve with tartar sauce.

Panfish with Parsley and Dill

8 crappies or sunfish, dressed (scale and remove heads, entrails, tails and fins; and drain.)

Cover bottom of baking dish with 1/4 cup finely chopped parsley and arrange the fish in the baking dish.

Top with:

2 tbsp. finely chopped parsley

2 tbsp. chopped fresh dill or

1 tsp. dill seed

Pour 1/4 cup hot water around the fish. Bake at 350° for 20 to 25 minutes and serve.

Pickled Northern Pike (or other fish)

Step #1: fillet the fish as you would a walleye--don't worry about the bones. Cut fish into small (herring-size) pieces. Wash.

Prepare a brine solution by adding one cup of salt (preferably pickling salt) to four cups of water.

Cover the fish pieces with the brine solution and let stand overnight.

Step #2: wash off the pieces of fish and soak in white vinegar three to four days.

Step #3: drain, rinse and place in jars (pint size is most convenient).

Prepare a pickling solution as follows:

To two cups of vinegar (if you like to use wine in cooking, use one cup of wine and one cup of vinegar) add -

one chopped onion (not fine)

one sliced lemon

2 tbsp. mustard seed (level)

1 3/4 cup sugar

4 bay leaves

5 whole cloves

1 tbsp. peppercorns (level)

5 or 6 small red peppers

1 tbsp. whole allspice

Bring the solution to a boil, then cool.

Step #4: pour the pickling solution over the fish pieces you have already packed in the jars (fairly tightly). Cover and refrigerate at least three to four days before serving.

Five to six pounds of cleaned and cut-up Northerns will yield approximately one gallon of pickled fish.

Shore Lunch

One of the most enjoyable meals on this earth is a shore lunch during a fishing trip!

Careful planning will mean far less time preparing the lunch. Be sure to include all necessary dishes, pans and utensils.

My favorite meal includes fried potatoes, beans, bread and, of course, freshly caught fish. Boil the potatoes (quartered) before you leave camp. Slice them into fries and keep them in a zip-lock bag. Plan 1 large potato per person. You will need a little oil to fry them. Chopped onion will enhance the potatoes but don't add the onion until you are ready to fry the potatoes.

A large can of beans will serve four. I like to "doctor" them with about a half-cup of ketchup and an equal amount of brown sugar. You can heat the beans and fry the potatoes while others are filleting the fish.

For enough fish to feed four, bring along 1/4 pound of cracker crumbs in a baggie; I crush them with a rolling pin before I leave camp. Mix in a generous amount of lemon pepper. If the crackers are salted, you won't need to salt the fish. Bring along an egg and a bowl in which to combine that egg with water. Dip the fillets in the egg wash and then in the crumbs and fry in oil on both sides until a golden brown. I use an iron skillet.

It is difficult to cook over an open fire, although it can be done if you bring along a grill to place on rocks over the fire. I prefer a Coleman gas stove.

Serve with bread and butter and cookies or bars for dessert.

And don't forget the beverage!

Game Birds

Half-Ducks on a Bed of Rice

    1 cup wild rice, washed

    2 ducks, halved lengthwise

    1/2 cup flour, seasoned with salt and pepper

    1 can cream of mushroom soup

    1 small can mushrooms (2 oz.)

    1 can water chestnuts, sliced

    1 cup sour cream or yogurt

    1 large onion, chopped

    1 cup celery, chopped

    2 tbsp. green pepper, chopped

    2 tbsp. orange peel

    salt and pepper to taste

Prepare the wild rice by any of the basic methods in the wild rice section which follows.

Halve the ducks with a stout knife or game shears.

Marinate the ducks overnight, refrigerated, breasts down, in the following solution:

    3 lemons, juice of

    1 large orange, juice of

    2 cups cider

    1/2 cup vinegar

    1 medium onion, chopped

    1/2 cup celery, chopped

    1 tsp. nutmeg

Roll the duck halves in flour and brown in cooking oil.

Prepare the rice bed by mixing together all ingredients. Season lightly with salt and pepper. Place all ingredients in a greased baking dish.

Lay the ducks on the rice bed, skin up. Roast uncovered in a 350° oven for 2 hours or until ducks are tender.

GOURMET ROAST DUCK WITH WILD RICE STUFFING AND HONEY GLAZE OR ORANGE SAUCE

Prepare the birds by scrubbing inside and out, being careful to trim away scraps of lung, etc.

Place in a large bowl, breasts down, and cover with cold water. Add two tbsp. salt per bird. Let stand in refrigerator overnight.

Prepare stuffing:

1 cup wild rice, washed

1-1/2 cups croutons

3/4 cup raisins

1/2 cup melted butter or margarine mixed with

1/2 cup hot water

1 large onion

1/3 pound chopped bologna or summer sausage or polish sausage or luncheon meat

Cook the wild rice according to one of the basic recipes in the wild rice section which follows.

Combine the rice, croutons, raisins, onion, and chopped meat. Season lightly with salt and pepper. Try to buy the preseasoned croutons, but if these aren't available or if you use dry bread, you may want to add a little sage seasoning.

Pour the melted butter-water mixture over the dressing and stir.

Take the birds out of salt water, pat dry with paper towel, season with salt and pepper, inside and out.

Stuff the birds loosely. Additional stuffing may be prepared in foil; place the package alongside the bird. If there isn't room in the roaster, just set it in the oven by itself. When prepared separately, the stuffing need not be in as long as the birds--about an hour will do.

Place the birds in roaster breast side up. Place a strip of fat bacon over each breast.

Add about one-half inch of water in bottom of roaster.

Cover and place in pre-heated low oven (250°). Bake three hours or until tender. Drumstick should wiggle easily.

Remove cover last half hour. Remove bacon strips and spread coat of honey over breasts to glaze during these last 30 minutes. Orange marmalade also forms a tasty glaze, or baste with orange sauce.

Prepared from:

2-1/2 tbsp. white sugar

1 cup brown sugar

1 tbsp. grated orange

1 cup orange juice (can be made from Tang or other powdered drink)

1 tbsp. cornstarch (dissolved in 1/3 cup hot water)

Combine the above ingredients and thicken in saucepan over medium-high heat; stir to prevent burning. For added zest, stir in a few drops of Tabasco sauce.

Duck Gravy

While duck is roasting, cook giblets (heart, gizzard and liver) by simmering in water until tender–about 1 hour.

Chop giblets.

Remove ducks from roaster.

Skim off the excess fat.

Using a spatula, carefully scrape loose the particles from the bottom on the pan. Do not scrape so hard as to loosen severely burned materials.

Using a pint jar with a cover as a shaker, add 1/2 cup water and 1/4 cup flour. Shake well. If a covered jar is not available, use a bowl, add flour and a little water to make a smooth paste. Now add the rest of the water and stir until the mixture is uniform and there are no lumps.

Remove roaster from heat. Add chopped giblets. Slowly stir in the flour and water mixture. Place roaster on low heat on top of stove and allow to simmer, stirring all the while. When the gravy is bubbling all over the roaster, add one tbsp. of Kitchen Bouquet and salt and pepper. Continue to stir over heat for another five minutes and serve. For thicker gravy, add more flour and water mixture.

Parboiled Ducks or Geese

Tough old ducks or geese will be made both tasty and tender by this technique.

Let ducks or geese stand in salted water overnight, breasts down (refrigerated).

Place birds in kettle, breasts down, cover with salted water. Bring to a boil; remove after about five to ten minutes of boiling. If you have reason to believe birds are tough, leave a little longer.

Remove ducks or geese from kettle, wash off any grease residue, salt and pepper inside and out.

Place ducks or geese in roaster, breast up, with a strip of bacon over each breast.

Place in pre-heated 250° oven and bake for another three hours. Remove cover last half hour to brown. Orange sauce (page 18), orange marmalade or honey glaze may be added at this time (remove bacon).

This technique is guaranteed to tenderize even the toughest old Greenhead!

Onion Soup Mix for Tough Old Birds

Fillet and dissect the duck, pheasant or goose and skin.

Do not season.

Lay pieces on foil in a single layer.

Place a generous pat of butter or margarine on each piece (about 1/4 pound per bird). Add about 2 tbsp. water.

Pour the dry onion soup mix over the meat pieces (one envelope for ducks or pheasant; two envelopes for a larger goose).

Fold the foil over the ducks and seal on top with your fingers.

Place in pre-heated 325° oven, sealed side up, for an hour and 15 minutes.

The soup mix liquid may be used as a gravy. Simply pour in bowl and add an equal amount of hot water.

Ducks, geese or pheasants you have had in the freezer for a long time are ideal candidates for this recipe.

Pheasant in Sour Cream

2 pheasants, cut into sections

1 small onion, diced

2 stalks celery, diced

2 cups sour cream

1/2 cup flour

2 tbsp. salt

1/2 tbsp. pepper

Dissect the birds including cutting the breasts of each bird into four pieces. Mix seasoning into flour and roll each piece therein. Brown slowly in frying pan. Sauté onions and celery pieces. Place pheasant in casserole. Mix onion and celery into sour cream and pour mixture over meat. Cover and bake in 325° oven for 1-1/2 to 2 hours or until tender.

Pheasant or Grouse Breasts with Wild Rice

1 cup wild rice, washed

4 pheasant breasts* (from 2 birds or 6 breasts from 3 grouse)

1 large onion, chopped

1 can golden cream of mushroom soup

1 cup sour cream

2 tbsp. green pepper, chopped

1/2 cup celery, chopped

1/8 pound butter

salt and pepper to taste

Cut breasts from carcass and marinade overnight, refrigerated, in the following solution:

15 whole cloves

8 bay leaves

8 peppercorns

1 large onion, chopped

1 cup white vinegar or cooking wine

1 cup water

Prepare the wild rice by any of the basic recipes in the wild rice section which follows.

Sauté the onion, green pepper, and celery a few minutes in butter over low heat.

Using the same butter, lightly brown the pheasant breasts.

Mix all ingredients and place in a greased casserole.

Lay the pheasant breasts on the bed of rice, skin side up, and bake uncovered, 1-1/2 hours in a 350° oven.

Meanwhile, prepare a sauce from the following:

1 cup cream

2 tbsp. white wine

2 chicken bouillon cubes

1 cup hot water

2 tsp. Worcestershire sauce

Heat sauce in a double broiler so that it will not scorch.

Serve one breast on a bed of rice on each plate. Spoon sauce over the pheasant and the rice.

*other parts of birds may be used in hot dishes, soups or stew.

Wild Rice and Grouse Cassrole

1 cup wild rice (washed)

flour

1 partridge, deboned and cut up into bite-size pieces

1 large onion, chopped

1 green pepper, chopped

1 small jar pimentos

1/2 cup celery, chopped

1 can mushroom soup

1 can water

salt and pepper

Prepare the wild rice by any of the recipes which follow in this section.

Cut the bird into bite-size pieces, removing all bones. Season, roll in flour and fry in oil slowly over low heat until browned but not "crusty". When it is about done, add the chopped onion, green pepper and celery. Continue frying for another three or four minutes. Add pimento, soup and water.

Place in a greased casserole. Cover and bake in a 300° oven for 1-1/2 hours. Add water while baking to prevent dryness.

This recipe works equally well with pheasant or chicken.

Game Animals

Big Game Stew

Ingredients to serve 6-8:

2 pounds roast meat. Bake until tender in a crockpot,* then cut into bite-size chunks. (Left-over roast also works well).

Prepare 1/2 cup wild rice by any of the methods that follow in this section.

In a large kettle, place:

2 cans vegetable beef stew

1 #2 can tomatoes

1 can mixed vegetables

2 small cans cream of tomato soup

the cooked wild rice

2 tbsp. catsup

Add the meat chunks and heat (about 30 minutes on a medium burner).

*I season the roast with pepper and garlic salt, then sear it in hot oil in a frying pan on both sides (about 1 minute per side). I then place it in a crock pot and add enough water to cover the roast and sprinkle an envelope of dry onion soup mix overall. After two hours I turn the roast over and bake another two hours on low heat.

Small Game Mulligan

Use whatever small game is available--squirrel, rabbit, partridge, pheasant, duck, etc. Don't hesitate to mix the game; the greater the variety the better.

Cut meat from the bone. Cut into bite-size chunks. Dredge in seasoned flour and brown in oil.

Cover with water, season with salt and pepper, and simmer 30 minutes. Then add the following:

1 #2 can tomatoes (or use fresh tomatoes)

1/2 cup wild rice, uncooked

1/2 cup catsup or two cans tomato soup (or some of each)

1 large onion, sliced

2 beef bouillon cubes (if no poultry meat is used, use 4 cubes and no chicken bouillon)

2 chicken bouillon cubes (if no red meat is used, use 4 cubes and no beef bouillon)

2 large carrots, sliced
1 turnip, sliced
3 large potatoes, cubed
1/2 cup celery, chopped
2 tbsp. parsley, chopped

Let simmer 3 hours. Pour off liquid or add water for desired "thickness". A crock pot works well for this recipe.

Jerky

Here's an entirely different taste treat from big game animals. Jerky makes a great snack and is also ideal for taking along on those outdoor excursions when you want something light but nutritious. American Indians and early white settlers used jerky extensively as a way of preserving meat.

The procedure for making jerky is simple, but it takes time:

Use only lean meat–trim away all the fat–and cut, with the grain–into strips one half inch thick and one inch wide. They may be of any length.

Mix together the following for each pound of meat strips:

2 tbsp. salt
1/4 tsp. cayenne pepper
1/2 tsp. black pepper
1 tbsp. sugar (preferably brown or maple)

If you like the flavor of garlic, add 1/2 tsp. garlic salt.

If you like a smoky flavor, add 1 tsp. liquid smoke.

Lay strips in a baking dish (glass or pottery–not metal), sprinkling the salt-pepper-sugar mixture generously over each layer.

Refrigerate for 1 day.

Dry each strip with paper towels and place on oven rack–with sides not touching or suspend each piece from the rack by running a toothpick through one end. Use a low oven, about 150° for 5 to 6 hours or until the meat is very dark in color–but not powdery or brittle.

Jerky may be stored in a cool, dry place without refrigeration.

Jerky may be broken into pieces and added to vegetables for a quick stew.

Wild Rice Recipes

Since nearly all recipes call for precooked wild rice, it is important that you develop your own, favorite method of preparation. With experience, the appearance of the rice will tell you when it is done; in the meantime, rely on taste. The kernels should not be hard, neither should they be mushy. If the rice is to be used in a recipe which calls for further cooking, it is better that it be a little undercooked.

In each recipe, it is important that the rice be washed thoroughly before cooking. A large sieve or colander works well.

One cup of wild rice yields about three cups of cooked rice.

Method #1

1. For most recipes, wash 1 cup wild rice.
2. About eight hours before you serve it or use it in another recipe, place the rice in a saucepan or kettle and cover it with about 1 quart of boiling water.
3. About 30 minutes before serving or using in another recipe, drain and rinse.
4. Cover with hot tap water, add 2 tsp. of salt, and let simmer until done (the rice is "flowered".)
5. Drain and fluff with a fork, adding salt and pepper to taste. If served as a side dish, add a pat of butter to each serving.

Method #2

1. Wash 1 cup rice.
2. Place in a saucepan or kettle and cover with 1 quart of water.
3. Add two level tsp. salt.
4. Bring to a boil.
5. Turn heat down, cover, and let simmer until the rice is well "flowered".
6. Fluff with a fork; let simmer a few more minutes until done to taste.
7. Drain; add butter, salt and pepper, fluff once more.

Method #3

1. Wash one cup wild rice; drain.
2. Place in saucepan or kettle, cover with water, and let stand overnight.
3. About 45 minutes before serving time (or using in another recipe), drain and cover with 1 quart boiling water.

4. Add 2 level tsp. salt.

5. Heat until it starts to boil again, then lower heat and let simmer, covered, for about 40 minutes or until rice is done to your taste. It should be "flowered".

6. Drain, add butter, and fluff with a fork.

Method #4

1. Wash one cup wild rice.

2. Place in a saucepan or kettle and cover with 1 quart boiling water.

3. Let stand, uncovered, 20 minutes.

4. Drain and repeat three more times. The last time, add two level tsp. of salt. After the last time the rice should be "flowered".

5. Drain, add butter, season to taste, and fluff with a fork.

Method #5

1. Wash 1 cup wild rice.

2. Place in a baking dish and cover with 1 quart of boiling water.

3. Add 1 tsp. salt.

4. Place in a pre-heated oven (350°).

5. After 1 hour, fluff with a fork. Add more water if necessary.

6. Continue baking another 20-30 minutes or until done to taste or the rice has "flowered".

7. Add a couple of pats of butter and fluff with a fork. Add salt and pepper to taste.

Wild Rice with Cream of Mushroom Soup

1 cup uncooked wild rice
1 can mushroom soup
1 small onion, chopped
1 cup celery, chopped
1 2 oz. can mushroom stems and pieces
1 small jar pimientos
1/2 small green pepper, chopped
1/3 cup slivered almonds or water chestnuts
salt and pepper to taste

Prepare the wild rice by any of the above basic recipes.
Sauté the chopped onion, celery, and green pepper a few minutes in oil or butter over low heat. Onions will appear "clear" when done.

Place the cooked rice in a greased casserole dish. Season lightly with salt and pepper. If salt was used in the basic preparation, be careful about adding too much.

Add the mushroom soup plus one can of water. Use the soup can to measure.

Add the celery, onions, green pepper, mushrooms, almonds, and pimientos. Stir together until thoroughly blended.

Bake in 300° oven, covered, for 1-1/2 hours. Check occasionally for dryness. Add water if necessary.

Serve as a vegetable or side dish.

Nutty Rice

1/2 cup uncooked wild rice
1 can chicken broth or chicken soup
1 small onion, chopped
1/2 cup celery, chopped
1/2 cup chopped nuts - not fine. Almonds, walnuts, hazelnuts, or cashews all work well-or even combinations
your favorite seasonings

Wash rice.

Cover rice with two cups hot water and let stand overnight or about 8 hours before using. About 1 hour before serving time, drain and cover with chicken broth or soup plus two cans of water-using the can to measure. Bring to a boil, then reduce heat and let simmer for 30 minutes or until rice is well flowered (better undercooked than overcooked at this point).

Meanwhile, sauté the onions and celery a few minutes or until the onion is clear.

Drain any excess liquid from the rice.

Place in a greased baking dish. Add onion, celery, and nuts. Lightly season with salt and pepper or your favorite seasonings, such as rosemary, thyme, parsley flakes, or marjoram. Stir together thoroughly.

Place covered dish in pre-heated oven (325°) for 20 minutes, fluffing with a fork once or twice in the process.

Wild Rice with Mushrooms

1 cup uncooked wild rice
1/2 stick butter (1/8 pound)
1/2 cup mushroom stems and pieces (either canned or uncooked)
salt and pepper to taste

Cook the wild rice by any of the basic recipes listed in this chapter, adding salt as directed.

When using uncooked mushrooms, add during last 30 minutes of cooking.

If using canned mushrooms, drain and add mushrooms during last few minutes of cooking.

When rice is done, shave butter stick into thin pats and stir in with fork as you fluff rice.

Add a little pepper and additional salt, if necessary, to taste.

If gravy is served with the meal, spoon a little over each serving.

Wild Rice and Sirloin*

2 cups rice
2 pounds sirloin steak
1 can golden mushroom soup
1 can cream of mushroom soup
1 small can mushrooms (4 oz.)
1/2 cup celery, chopped
1 cup onion, chopped
1/4 cup soy sauce
1 cup commercial sour cream
1 cup half and half
1/2 cup slivered almonds (use some in hot dish and balance as garnish)
2 tsp. salt
1/4 pound butter

Prepare wild rice by any of the basic methods in this chapter.

Cut sirloin into small chunks and sauté in butter. Add celery, onion, soups, salt, mushrooms, and sour cream. Bring to a gentle boil. Remove from heat. Add part of the almonds.

Place wild rice in a buttered 3 quart casserole. Pour the hot mixture over the rice. Toss lightly. Bake about 1 hour in 350° oven. Add some half and half if needed. Keep plenty moist and stir one or two times during baking process.

Garnish with slivered almonds.

*Courtesy Avis Sandland, Clearbrook, MN

Creamy Mushroom Wild Rice Soup

1/3 cup wild rice, washed
2 cans cream of mushroom soup
1/4 pound fresh mushrooms, sliced (or 1-2 oz. can)
1/2 cup celery, chopped
1 can chicken broth or 2 chicken bouillon cubes and 1 cup hot water
1 carrot, sliced thin
2 cups half and half
1/4 pound bacon bits, fried but not crisp
1 tsp. salt
pepper (to taste)
1/8 pound butter

Prepare the wild rice by any of the basic recipes listed earlier in this chapter.
Fry the bacon pieces, but not crisp.
Sauté the onion and celery in the butter a few minutes or until onion is clear.
Combine all ingredients in a soup pot, bring to a low boil, reduce heat, and let simmer 1 hour.

Wild Rice Bread*

1/2 cup wild rice
1 package dry yeast
1/4 cup warm water
1/4 cup brown sugar
1/2 cup molasses
1/4 cup butter, softened
2-1/2 cups boiled - cooled water
1 tbsp. salt
1/2 cup potato buds
7 to 8 cups all purpose flour

Prepare wild rice by any of the basic methods in this chapter.
Dissolve the yeast in the quarter cup warm water.
Using a warm bowl, add the 2-1/2 cups of cooled water, the yeast mixture, brown sugar, molasses, salt, butter, potato buds and 2 cups of flour. Beat until smooth.
Add the cooked rice (drained) and balance of flour to make a soft dough.

Turn onto a floured board and knead for ten minutes.

Place in a greased bowl, cover and let rise in a warm place until about double the original volume (about 2 hours).

Divide into 4 parts and form into loaves. Place in greased bread pans.

Cover again and let rise until almost double in bulk.

Bake 30 to 35 minutes in a 350° oven.

Cool on wire rack.

Especially good served with cheese whip and olives.

*Courtesy Avis Sandland, Clearbrook, MN

THE WOODLANDS AS OUR GARDEN

Mushrooms (WARNING!!!)

We shall make no attempt here to offer guidance in the picking of mushrooms. The printed page, and even pictures, are no guarantee you will avoid poisonous varieties. We suggest you apprentice yourself to a veteran mushroom picker and learn first-hand.

Morel Mushrooms

Morels need not be peeled. The whole mushroom is edible. Do not soak morels, must brush away any dust or dirt and cut any defective parts. The lower part of the stalk may be a little tougher and can be removed. The best parts will cut crisp but tender. Slice the mushroom into bite-size pieces and sauté in butter until wilted and tender–not browned.

Salt and serve with steaks or chops.

Morels may be canned, frozen or dehydrated.

Puff Ball Mushrooms

Wash the puff balls, but do not soak. Cut away any defective parts. Slice and dip pieces in your favorite chicken or fish batter. Deep fry. Small puff balls may be fried whole. Pieces may be added (raw) to stews or gravies during the last few minutes of cooking.

This variety may be canned, frozen or dehydrated.

Shelf Fungus

Cut away any defective or woody parts.

Slice into convenient cooking size.

Sauté in butter or deep-fry coated with your favorite batter.

Shelf fungus may be canned, but may not be frozen or dehydrated.

Baked Mushrooms

1 pound thickly sliced mushrooms
1/2 cup chopped onions
2 tbsp. lemon juice
1/2 cup butter
2 tbsp. flour
1/3 cup grated cheese
1/2 cup sour cream
1/2 cup dry bread crumbs
salt and pepper

Sauté the mushroom slices with the onions and lemon juice in the butter. When the onions are clear (3 or 4 minutes) season with salt and pepper (lightly) and stir in the flour while still over heat.
Place in a baking dish.
Combine the grated cheese and sour cream and spoon over the mushroom mixture. Sprinkle with bread crumbs and top with a few dabs of butter.
Bake in a hot oven (375-400°) for 15 minutes or until a light, golden brown.

Mushroom Stuffing for Fish or Fowl

3 cups seasoned croutons (or 2 cups cooked wild rice and 1 cup croutons)
1 cup chopped celery
1 cup chopped onion
1/4 pound butter or margarine
1 cup sliced mushrooms (need not be precooked, but may be)
salt and pepper
1/2 cup hot water

Sauté the onions and celery over low heat (in butter) until clear. Add the hot water and pour entire mixture over croutons and/or wild rice. Add mushrooms and season. Stir together. Stuff fowl or fish lightly (do not pack).

WARNING!
Do not stuff fish until just before it is placed in the oven. If stuffing is placed in fish or birds prior to baking, poisons may develop.

WILD FRUITS AND BERRIES

Wild fruits and berries are usually more flavorful than their cultivated counterparts; however, they tend to be more tart and therefore will require more sugar than traditional recipes. Otherwise, your favorite treatments for sauces, pies, jellies and jams will work very well. Most of the recipes found in this chapter are appropriate for nearly all of the wilderness fruits and berries, including chokecherries, blueberries, raspberries, strawberries, blackberries and June berries.

Chokecherry Syrup

Great on pancakes, waffles, or French toast or as a topping for ice cream.

4 cups berries

2 cups water

2 cups sugar

Place berries and water together in a kettle; bring to a boil, reduce heat so that the liquid will boil slowly until the chokecherries are soft. Force the mixture through a sieve. Stir in sugar and return to stove; let simmer, stirring constantly until it thickens. Remember the thickening will increase as the mixture cools. Pour into sterilized glass jars and seal. If the syrup will be kept under refrigeration or in a cool place, an ordinary screw cap such as found on mayonnaise jars will suffice.

This recipe also works well with most other berries but in the case of blueberries or strawberries, for example, you may prefer not to strain out the pulp.

Chokecherry and Wine Jelly

1 cup Chokecherry juice (or use 2 cups of chokecherry syrup and omit the sugar)

1 cup red wine

3 cups sugar

1/2 bottle liquid pectin

To make the juice, cover the berries with water, bring to a boil and then let simmer until the berries soften. Force through a sieve or jelly bag.

Mix the juice, wine and sugar in a kettle until the sugar dissolves.

Bring to a boil as you stir; let boil 1 minute (continue stirring).

Remove from the stove and gradually stir in the pectin. Ladle into preheated jars or jelly glasses.

Seal (paraffin will do).

Blueberry Jelly*

2 cups juice (make juice by following procedure explained above for chokecherries)
4 cups sugar
1 tsp. lemon juice (or whatever citrus juice you have handy)
1 bottle fruit pectin

Stir the juice, sugar and lemon juice together until the sugar dissolves. Bring to a boil. Add a restaurant size pat of butter to reduce foaming. Stir constantly. After the mixture comes to a full boil, remove from heat and add pectin. Return to the stove and let boil 1 minute, stirring all the while. Skim off any foam. Ladle into heated sterilized jelly glasses and seal with paraffin.

Blueberry Jam

4 cups cleaned blueberries
5 cups sugar
1 cup water

Mix together the above ingredients. Bring to a boil and then reduce heat so that it will boil slowly, for 15 minutes or until thick. Stir all the while, crushing the berries occasionally with a spoon. If the mixture is too dry at any point to boil freely, add a little water.
Ladle into sterilized glasses or jars and seal.

Blueberry Sauce

Most any wild berries may be used with this updated version of an old favorite recipe.

4 cups berries (carefully picked over and cleaned)
2/3 cup sugar
3 tbsp. corn starch (flour may be substituted)
2 cups water (hot)
2 tbsp. lemon or other citrus juice
1/2 tsp. salt
2 pats butter

Combine the sugar, cornstarch and salt.

Add the lemon juice to the hot water. Stir this mixture, a little at a time, into the dry mixture. When it is smooth, place over low heat and cook until it thickens, stirring occasionally.

Add blueberries and continue simmering until the sauce has the desired "thickness", remembering that it will thicken still more as it cools.

Remove from the stove and stir in the butter as it melts.

This also makes an excellent syrup; just continue the heating and stirring process until it is "syrupy".

Blueberry pie recipe may be found on page 58.

Blueberry Muffins

Ingredients for 20-22 muffins

Cream together 1/2 cup butter (or margarine), 1-1/8 cup sugar and two eggs. Add 1 cup sour cream (can use no fat) or plain yogurt, 1 tsp. vanilla, 2 cups of flour, 1 tsp. baking powder, 1/2 tsp. baking soda and 1/4 tsp. salt. Stir in a cup fresh blueberries. Bake 20 minutes at 400° in muffin tins. Sprinkle with powdered sugar.

Courtesy Carolyn Ring, Turtle Lake, Bemidji, MN

Wild Cranberries

Minnesota has hundreds of wild cranberry bogs hidden away in tamarack and spruce swamps. Finding them is a real challenge, and don't count on anyone showing you their favorite spot! The cranberries are often hidden under the foliage and defy detection. Oh yes, you'll need a pair of hip boots!

Once you find the cranberries, you may cook them with the very same recipes you use for those purchased in the supermarket. Here are a few that may be new to you, however:

Cranberry Relish

Wash the berries and let dry.

Put them through a grinder or chopper, making a cranberry pulp.

For each cup of pulp add 1 cup of sugar. Stir until the sugar is completely blended into the pulp.

For a more tart flavor, add 2 tbsp. lemon or orange juice for each cup of pulp.

Serve with any wild game, but what could be better than wild cranberries with wild turkey or duck?

Cranberry Stuffing

Use your favorite stuffing recipe but add one cup chopped raw cranberries.

Pincherry Jelly

Extract the juice by adding 3 cups of water to 2 cups of berries. Simmer about 5 minutes as you mash the berries. Strain through a jelly bag or sieve.

Return the juice to the stove and bring to a boil. Then lower the temperature and let simmer 15 minutes, stirring regularly.

Remove from heat and add 1 bottle fruit pectin. Skim off foam and ladle into hot jelly glasses. Seal with paraffin.

The jelly will be clear and a very bright red.

A cup of red wine added during the last 15 minutes of simmering will give the jelly an exciting taste.

Spicy Jams and Jellies

Add 1/2 tsp. each of:
ground cloves
ground allspice
ground cinnamon

before the final boiling or simmering process starts. The spicy taste goes especially well with blueberry and rose hip jellies.

Mixed Fruit Jellies

The juices of some berries and fruits may be combined to attain special textures and flavors. For example, apple juice may be added to chokecherries, wild plums, rose hips or wild grapes. Don't be afraid to experiment.

A combination that will have your family and guests guessing is to use equal parts of most any berry juice and sumac juice. To extract sumac juice, cover the red berries with water and boil a few minutes and then strain.

Sumac has been called the "lemonade of the wilderness".

Wild Plum Butter

Wash and remove blemished or spoiled areas.

Make plum pulp by covering the fruit with water (just barely) and then boil until the plums are soft. Force through a sieve or food mill.

To each cup of pulp, add 2/3 cup of sugar. Cook until thick, stirring regularly. It should take about a half-hour.

Ladle into pre-heated glasses and seal.

For a little spicier flavor, add a tbsp. of cinnamon and a tbsp. of cloves to each cup of pulp before cooking.

Part II

Traditional Minnesota Cooking

This section includes traditional Minnesota dishes, the kind served at church suppers and found in those wonderful cookbooks published by church groups, service clubs and other organizations.

MINNESOTA BREAKFASTS

Pancakes from Scratch

Ingredients to serve 4:

2 cups flour
1-3/4 cups milk
2 heaping tbsp. baking powder
2 eggs (beat separately)
1/8 pound (1/2 stick) melted butter
3 tbsp. sugar
1 tbsp. (level) salt

Sift all dry ingredients into a bowl. Add eggs (already beaten) to milk and mix thoroughly. Add the milk-egg mixture to the dry ingredients - slowly - stirring as you add. Continue stirring until relatively smooth, but don't worry about small lumps. Add melted butter (or shortening) and fry on a hot griddle.

A few tips to guarantee success

For richer, more attractive looking cakes, add one more egg.
You will have to learn the right consistency through experience, but beware of heavy batter - the cakes will be too thick and may not get done in the center. Strive for thin, light cakes - about 1/3 inch thick.
Use a hot griddle, lightly greased. Drops of water will "dance" on the surface when it is ready.
Make cakes about 4 to 6 inches in diameter. Never make large pancakes; they tend to be tough on the outside and raw in the center.
Turn the cakes when bubbles appear in the batter.
Turn the cakes only once to avoid making them tough.

Gourmet Cakes

Use previous recipe and simply do one or more (or all) of the following:

Add fruit, such as blueberries, to the batter.
Add pre-fried, small pieces of bacon.
Serve with hot syrup. Always remove the cap before heating! Place the syrup bottle in a pan of hot water. Never heat any container (can, plastic, or glass) without first removing the cover or at least puncturing the top. It will prevent an explosion!

Waffles

Use any pancake recipe, but make the batter a little heavier than for pancakes.
For a richer batter, substitute light cream for the milk.
Pre-heat the waffle iron until it is steaming hot. Grease the iron lightly (both surfaces) with cooking oil, butter, or margarine to prevent sticking (not necessary with newer, non-stick irons).
Pour on the batter, not quite covering the entire surface; it will expand. Let stand about 30 seconds before closing the lid.
When the iron stops steaming or the light goes out it will be done. Peek cautiously to be sure!
Serve with plenty of butter or margarine and warm syrup.

French Toast

Always a favorite and a good way to use up leftover bread. In fact, fresh bread does not make as good French toast as older bread. To coat eight to ten pieces you will need:

4 eggs
1 cup of water (or milk)
4 heaping tbsp. pancake mix
Combine the eggs and water in a bowl with an electric mixer or hand-propelled egg beater (or a fork and lots of elbow grease). If you prefer a light coating on the toast, do not add the pancake flour; if you prefer a heavier batter, then beat the flour into the mixture. Try it both ways and with more or less flour until you get the consistency you like. You might also try both milk and water; however, the milk may give the toast a slightly "scorched" flavor.
Fry the toast on a hot griddle or in a skillet.
Either way, use plenty of oil.

Scrambled Eggs

Place the eggs in a bowl and stir with a fork until the yolks and whites are thoroughly blended. Add a tbsp. of water for every two eggs. Pour the mixture into a pre-heated, greased frying pan or onto a griddle.

Stir occasionally with your spatula until done. Again, cook them long enough so they are not "watery" but not so long that they get "rubbery." Season lightly and serve.

To make your eggs go farther, stir in small chunks of bread (about 1/2 inch square) before you fry the eggs.

An entirely different taste is achieved by breaking the eggs directly into the pan and stirring gently as they fry.

Minnesota Skillet Breakfast #1

Ingredients to serve 4:

6 medium red potatoes, cut into small bite-size chunks
8 eggs, beaten
1 pound pork sausage (bulk type)
1 medium onion, peeled and chopped
1 cup cheddar cheese, grated or shredded
2 tbsp. vegetable oil
salt and pepper to taste

Cook the potato chunks in water in a covered sauce pan for about 20 minutes or until soft.

Meanwhile, brown the crumbled sausage and chopped onion in vegetable oil in skillet.

When the potatoes are done, add them and the beaten eggs to the skillet. Season lightly with salt and pepper and then stir all ingredients together in the pan.

Cook over medium plus heat, stirring regularly, until eggs are cooked.

Sprinkle cheese on top and place under a broiler a couple of minutes or until cheese is melted.

Serve in pie shaped pieces. (cut with a knife and remove from the skillet with a spatula).

Minnesota Skillet Breakfast #2

Ingredients to serve 4:

1 pkg. frozen hashbrowns, thawed
8 eggs
1-1/2 cups pre-cooked ham, diced
1 medium onion, peeled and chopped
salt and pepper to taste
1-1/2 cups shredded or grated cheese of your choosing
3 tbsp. vegetable oil

Sauté the onion, ham and hashbrowns in oil in a skillet; stirring regularly for about 10 minutes over medium heat.
Beat the eggs. Stir in about 1/2 tsp. pepper and 1/4 tsp. salt. Stir eggs into the contents of the skillet and continue cooking until the eggs solidify.
Sprinkle cheese over skillet contents and place briefly under a broiler until the cheese melts. Watch carefully; it should only take a minute or two.

Lake of the Woods Omelet

Serves 4:

9 large eggs
2 tbsp. chopped onions (heaping)
8 slices bacon - cut into 1/2" pieces and pre-fried
3 tbsp. chopped cheese (American or Cheddar)
2 tbsp. water

Use a non-stick frying pan. Use medium-high heat. Coat the bottom of the pan with butter or margarine. The size of the pan you use is important, because the egg mixture should be about one-half inch deep when it has been poured into the pan. By covering the pan, you will assure more uniform cooking throughout the omelet. Combine all ingredients in the skillet. When the omelet is well browned on the bottom (about four minutes), flip it over. If you are using a larger skillet (you can easily make as many as six portions in a medium skillet) cut the omelet into pie-shaped, individual servings before turning. Make the cut with the edge of your spatula and turn one portion at a time. The process may seem a little "messy" because the surface of the omelet will be runny while the bottom is already firm.

But it will surprise you how well it will work out - just so the bottom of the omelet is done well enough to hold together as you turn it over.

Salt and pepper lightly before the omelet leaves the pan. Each can add seasoning to suit his own taste at the table. Be sure to have the catsup bottle handy for those who want added spice.

Some prefer to fold the omelet when it is served and put some of the ingredients (pre-heated) into the fold - such as sliced mushrooms or chopped ham. A couple of spoonfuls of jam or jelly placed in the fold will also add flavor and prevent your omelet from tasting dry. Folded omelets require a smaller pan (single portion size) and a thinner omelet. In fact, omelet "purists" will insist that omelets should be prepared as individual portions.

Blueberry Muffins #2

1 egg
1/2 tbsp. butter (melted)
2 cups flour
3-1/2 tbsp. baking powder
1 cup milk
1/2 tbsp. salt
2 tbsp. sugar
1 cup blueberries

Add the baking powder and salt to the two cups of sifted flour (sift before measuring). Now place the milk in a bowl and add the sugar. Beat the egg into the milk; melt the butter and add it to the milk-egg mixture. Sift the dry ingredients into the liquid mixture. Add the blueberries and stir gently until the ingredients are uniformly dampened. Don't worry about the lumps in the mixture.

Pour the ingredients into a muffin pan and bake in a moderate oven for about twenty-five minutes or until a toothpick thrusts easily into the muffin and they are well browned.

SOUPS

Beer Cheese Soup

Ingredients to serve 4:

1/4 pound (1 stick) butter or margarine or 8 tbsp. oil
1/2 tsp. seasoned salt
1/2 tsp. celery salt
1 tsp. Worcestershire sauce
1/2 cup diced onion
1/4 cup diced celery
1/2 cup flour
2 cans condensed chicken broth
1 can (12 oz.) beer
2 cups shredded cheddar cheese
popcorn for garnish (optional but traditional)

Melt butter in a large saucepan; add seasonings; onions and celery.
Cook over medium heat until vegetables are softened. Add flour,
whisking to blend. Cook until bubbly; reduce heat to low and add
remaining ingredients, whisking until cheese melts.
Garnish with popcorn.

Baked Potato Soup

Ingredients to serve 8:

5 medium baked potatoes (skin may be left on) diced
1 medium onion, chopped
2 ribs celery, chopped
1 clove garlic, minced
1 can cream of chicken soup
1 can cream of celery soup
2 cans water
1 cup cream
1/8 pound butter or margarine (1/2 stick) or 4 tbsp. oil
6 slices bacon, fried or broiled crisp and broken into bits
1/4 pound cheddar cheese, shredded or grated
salt and pepper to taste

Bake potatoes, let cool, cut into small chunks.

Sauté the onion, celery and garlic in the melted butter a few minutes or until onion is translucent. Combine all ingredients (except bacon and cheese) in a soup pot. Simmer over low heat for 20 minutes; do not boil. Meanwhile, fry or broil bacon and break into bits. Serve soup piping hot with cheese and bacon on surface as garnish.

Barley with Beef and Vegetables Soup

Ingredients to serve 6:

1-1/2 pounds beef stew meat, cut bit-size
1 cup chopped cabbage
1 qt. water
1 medium onion, peeled and chopped
1 can tomatoes, Italian style, chopped (save liquid)
2/3 cup pearl barley
1 medium potato, peeled and chopped
1/8 pound butter or margarine (1/2 stick) melted or 4 tbsp. oil
1 carrot, sliced thin
2 ribs celery, chopped
3 tbsp. catsup (for seasoning)

Sauté the onion, celery and garlic a few minutes until onion is translucent. Place in a large soup pot. Add water, beef, tomatoes and catsup. Bring to a boil, then reduce heat and simmer 1-1/2 to 2 hours or until meat is tender.

At this point you may need to add more water. Add carrots, potatoes and barley and continue to simmer for 20 minutes. Add cabbage and let simmer another 15-20 minutes or until everything is tender.

Fresh Garden Tomato Soup

Ingredients to serve 4-6:

4 large tomatoes, peeled and diced
1/8 pound butter or margarine (1/2 stick) or 4 tbsp. oil
8 leeks, chopped - white part only
2 ribs celery, chopped
2 cloves garlic, minced
4 tbsp. tomato paste
2 cups water

2 cups chicken broth
2 tbsp. catsup
6 drops Tabasco sauce
4 tbsp. chives, chopped for garnish (or parsley)

Sauté the onions, celery and garlic a few minutes or until onion is translucent.
Combine all ingredients in a soup pot (except the garnish). Bring to a boil, then reduce heat to simmer and cook 20 minutes.
Garnish with chives or parsley.

SALADS

Caramel Apple Salad*

Ingredients to serve 8:

1 jumbo egg white
1-1/2 cup powdered sugar
3/4 cup softened butter
6 oz. sour cream

Cream the above ingredients together.

8 oz. Kool Whip
4 large Granny Smith apples chopped
32 oz. crushed pineapple
8 oz. lightly salted peanuts (chopped or whole)

Gradually add the above four items.
Refrigerate

Frog Eyed Salad*

Ingredients for 6:

1/2 # (1# package) "Acini Di Pepe" pasta - cook and drain
1 egg, beat until foamy

1/2 cup sugar

1 tbsp. flour
1/4 tsp. salt

Stir in the above three items with the reserved pineapple juice, cook over low heat and stir until thickened and bubbly.

1 15 oz. can crushed pineapple (reserve juice and use above)
1 16 oz. can fruit cocktail
1 cup miniature marshmallows
1 cup whipping cream - whipped

Mix pasta and egg mixture. Chill thoroughly, about 1 hour. Stir in fruit and marshmallows. Fold in whipped cream. Cover and chill. Stir before serving.

Courtesy Betsy Hayenga, Lake Alexander, Cushing, MN

HOT DISHES

No book on Minnesota cooking would be complete without a section on hot dishes. Not only are they important family fare, but the famous Minnesota potluck suppers would be dull without them.

Hamburger Hot Dish with Mushrooms

Ingredients:

1 pound hamburger
2 cans cream of mushroom soup
2 cans water
1 cup chopped celery
1 cup chopped onion
1/2 cup rice (uncooked)
1 tbsp. soy sauce
1/2 cup canned mushrooms or 1 cup fresh

Brown the hamburger in a well greased skillet. Combine all ingredients in a buttered casserole dish and bake in a pre-heated 350° oven for 1 hour.
(8 oz. of noodles may be substituted for the rice, but cook them first according to directions on the package.)

Hamburger-Tomato Hot Dish

Same recipe as above but replace mushroom soup with 2 cans tomatoes and do not add mushrooms.

Wild Rice and Hamburger Hotdish

1 cup wild rice (washed)
1 lb. hamburger (beef or wild game)
1 large onion, chopped
1 cup celery, chopped
1 small green pepper, chopped
1 small jar pimientos
1 can mushroom soup
1 can water

Prepare the rice by any recipe in Part I.

Fry the hamburger, use a little oil so it will not burn.
When it is about done, add the chopped onion, celery and green pepper. Continue frying for another three or four minutes.
Add pimiento, soup and water.
Mix in wild rice.
Place in a buttered casserole dish.
Bake 1-1/2 hours in a 300° oven. Add water while baking to prevent dryness.

Corned Beef Hot Dish

Ingredients to serve 6:

8 oz. egg noodles - cooked
1 can corned beef - break apart
1/4 # American cheese - diced
2 cans cream of chicken soup
1/2 cup diced onion
1 cup diced celery
1 cup milk
pepper
3/4 cup buttered crumbs on top

Bake in a 350° oven, uncovered.

Calico Beans Hot Dish *

Ingredients to serve 8:

1/4 pound bacon - cut up
1 lb. hamburger
1/2 cup chopped onion
1/2 cup brown sugar
1/2 cup catsup
2 tbsp. vinegar
1 tbsp. prepared mustard
1 can kidney beans
1 can lima beans
4 cups baked beans

Brown together (in oil) the first three items (bacon, hamburger and onions).
Bake in a slow oven one to two hours.

* Courtesy Betsy Hayenga, Lake Alexander, Cushing, MN

Hamburger and Noodle Hot Dish with Peas

Ingredients:

8 oz. noodles (1/2 package)
1 pound ground beef
1 can onion rings
1 cup chopped onion
1/2 cup chopped celery
1 can cream of celery soup
1/2 can water
1 can peas (drained)

Brown the ground beef in a well-greased skillet. Combine all ingredients in a buttered casserole dish (except the onion rings); scatter the onion rings on top. Bake 30 minutes in a pre-heated 350° oven.

Fish and Potato Hot Dish

Ingredients to serve 4:

2 pounds of fillets. Almost any variety, but salmon and lake trout are
especially good
6 potatoes, sliced
butter, enough to butter the casserole dish
3 tbsp. chopped dill or 2 tbsp. dill seed
salt and pepper
6 eggs
1 pint of milk (2 cups)

Butter the casserole dish. Place a layer of sliced potatoes on the
bottom. Next a layer of fillets. Lightly season the fillets with salt and
pepper. Sprinkle lightly with the dill. Add another layer of potatoes;
then a layer of fish, more seasonings, etc. making sure the top layer is
potatoes. Beat the eggs and milk together and pour over all. Bake in a
low oven (250°) for about 1 hour or until potatoes are done.

Tunafish Hot Dish

Ingredients:

1 standard size can of tuna
1 onion (medium) chopped quite fine
2 tbsp. chopped green pepper
1 can mushroom soup
1 cup cheese (Velveeta or similar)
2 eggs
1/2 package egg noodles (8 oz.)

Cook egg noodles in water according to package directions. Mix
together all ingredients, place in a greased casserole dish, and bake for
45 minutes in a pre-heated 350° oven.

Sweet Potato Hot Dish

1-23 oz. can serves four if used as an "extra" vegetable; otherwise, use
two cans.
Empty can into a well greased casserole or baking dish. Mash the
potatoes level with a fork. Add a chunk of margarine or butter here
and there.

Cover, and bake in a pre-heated 300° oven for about 45 minutes.

Remove the cover and spread a layer of marshmallows (small size works better) over the surface of the sweet potatoes.

Return to the oven for a few minutes (uncovered) until marshmallows have melted together and turned a light brown. If you are in a hurry, brown marshmallows by using the "over-head" broiler in your oven.

Cheesy Vegetarian Hot Dish

Ingredients to serve 6:

3 large potatoes, peeled and chunked bite-size
1 medium cabbage (about 2#) cut into bite-size chunks (discard core and outer portions)
1 large parsnip, peeled and sliced thin
1 large turnip, peeled and sliced thin
1 large carrot, scraped and sliced thin
1 medium rutabaga, peeled and diced
1 large onion, peeled, sliced and broken into rings
1/2 stick butter, melted and divided
1/2 tsp. salt
1/4 tsp. pepper
1-1/2 cups cheddar cheese, grated or shredded

Cover the potatoes, cabbage, carrot, rutabaga, turnip and parsnip pieces with water in a sauce pan and boil, covered, until the vegetables start to soften. Using a slotted spoon, remove the cabbage after 3 minutes, all of the vegetables except the potatoes after 5 minutes and remove the potatoes after 10 minutes.

Sauté the onion rings in a skillet in 1/2 of the butter.

Place all of the ingredients, including the melted butter in a lightly greased baking dish or pan. Season with salt and pepper as you stir them together but save 1/2 cup of grated cheese to sprinkle on top. Bake in a pre-heated 350° oven covered, one hour.

Walleye and Potato Hot Dish

Ingredients to serve 4:

4 walleye fillets, about 8 oz. each
4 large potatoes, peeled and sliced - about 1/2 inch thick
1 small onion, peeled, sliced and broken into rings
1 cup milk

2 tbsp. minced, fresh dill
4 tbsp. grated Parmesan cheese
1/2 tsp. salt
1/4 tsp. pepper
lemon pepper

In a sauce pan, cover the potato slices with water and boil (covered) 15 minutes or until they just start to soften. Drain and cool to handle.

Using a lightly greased 12x12 baking dish or pan, layer the potato slices on the bottom. Pour the milk over the potatoes. Layer the onion rings on top of the potatoes. Lightly season with salt and pepper.

Lay the 4 fish fillets on top of the onion rings side by side. Season with lemon pepper. Sprinkle with chopped dill. Sprinkle with Parmesan cheese (about 1 tbsp. per fillet).

Bake, uncovered, in a 350° oven 20 minutes or until the fish flakes with a fork. Do not over-cook.

Pheasant, Partridge, Cornish Game Hen or Duck and Wild Rice Hot Dish

1 game bird, well baked, seasoned with salt and pepper, basted with soy sauce, and cut up into bite-size chunks
1 cup wild rice, well washed
1 stick butter (1/4 pound)
2 cups diced celery
1 medium onion, chopped
1 large can mushroom pieces
1 can mushroom soup
4 tbsp. soy sauce (plus soy sauce for basting bird)

Prepare wild rice by any of the basic methods in Part I.

Roast bird, seasoned with salt and pepper and basted with soy sauce, until well done. Cut into bite-size pieces.

In a pan, sauté the celery and onion pieces in butter. Add the meat pieces, stock from the roasting pan, drained mushrooms, mushroom soup, and 4 tbsp. soy sauce. Stir together.

Place all of the above ingredients, plus the wild rice, in a buttered baking dish--mix together well.

Dab with butter and sprinkle a little soy sauce on top.

Bake in a 350° oven for 20-25 minutes.

Makes about 6 servings. If the birds are small, use two.

Sauerkraut with Meat Hot Dish

Ingredients:

1 large can sauerkraut
1 can water
2 tbsp. brown sugar
8 wieners or 1/2 pound side pork
2 medium potatoes, peeled and grated

Combine the sauerkraut, water and sugar and simmer over low heat 30 minutes. If you used wieners, cut them into chunks and add them to the sauerkraut at the start. If you choose side pork, fry it first and add it to the kraut after it has been cooked. Add the grated potatoes, stirring them in and continue to cook another 30 minutes our until the mixture starts to thicken.

Serve as is or over boiled potatoes.

Spam Hot Dish

Ingredients:

1 can of Spam, ground or chopped fine
1 can cream of mushroom soup
1 can cream of chicken soup
1 cup cheese, chopped fine (Velveeta type)
1 can condensed milk (or half and half)
3 tbsp. chopped onion
8 oz. (half-package) macaroni

Prepare macaroni according to directions on the package; drain. Combine all ingredients in a buttered casserole dish and bake about 45 minutes in a pre-heated 350° oven.

TRADITIONAL MEAT RECIPES

Roasts

Good quality and tender roasts of beef, pork or wild game.

Rub roast with salt, pepper and garlic salt.
Place on a rack in a shallow pan - fat side up (with wild game, remove fat and lay a couple of pieces of fat bacon on top).
Leave pan uncovered; do not add water.
Place in pre-heated medium oven (300-325°).

Allow

28-30 minutes per pound for rare
32-35 minutes per pound for medium
37-40 minutes per pound for well done

It is a good idea to use a thermometer. It is easy to spoil a roast by having it either too well done or uncooked in the center.
A meat thermometer will read:

140° for rare
160° for medium
170° for well done (never exceed this temperature)

All Purpose Gravy Recipe

After you remove the roast, skim most of the fat from the remaining meat stock.

Using a covered pint jar for a shaker, add 1/2 cup of water and 1/4 cup of flour. Shake until well mixed. If you don't have a jar, use any small container. Place the flour in the container and add a little water. Using a spoon, make a smooth paste. Now add the balance of the water and stir until well blended - no lumps.

Remove the stock from the heat and slowly stir in the flour and water mixture. Return to the stove and simmer, Meanwhile stirring constantly. When the gravy is bubbling all over in the pan, add a tablespoon of Kitchen Bouquet. Add salt and pepper; continue to stir for another five minutes.

STEAKS

Broiled

Use thick cuts (3/4 inch to 1 inch)

If you are using venison or other wild game, trim away all fat.

Broil over hot coals or gas. When the steak is well-browned, turn it over. The degree of doneness depends, of course, on two factors: heat and time. Because everyone has his own preference (rare, medium rare, medium, well done, etc.) and because the heat will vary with each grill, there is no time formula; but for a starter, try 8 minutes on a side for medium rare. You will have to learn by experience with each grill; outside appearances of a steak are deceiving.

Just remember - the hotter the charcoal or broiler the better.

Place the orders for "well-done" on first and the orders for rare on last so that the steaks will all be ready at the same time.

Apply seasoning after you turn the steaks and turn with tongs rather than a fork.

Baked Mushroom Style

Arrange the steaks in a single layer in a baking dish or oven pan. An iron skillet will do, providing it does not have a wood or plastic handle. Season lightly with salt and pepper.

Cover the steaks with mushroom soup. One 26 oz. can of soup plus one can of water will cover two pounds of steaks. Be sure the liquid covers the meat.

Add as many fresh or canned mushrooms as you like.

Cover the pan or dish. If you do not have a cover that fits, use foil. Place in pre-heated, 300° oven. Bake for two hours.

Swiss Steak (Tomato Style)

2 pounds round steak (if wild game, trim away fat)

1 can tomato soup

1 can water

1 can tomato sauce

1 cup chopped celery
1 large sliced onion
1 small, sliced green pepper
salt and pepper

Season steaks and arrange in single layer in baking dish or pan.
Add chopped celery, sliced onion and sliced green pepper.
Cover with soup mixture (tomato soup and equal amount of water). Be sure meat is covered by liquid. If you prefer a spicier sauce, add catsup or a couple of drops of Tabasco sauce. Place in pre-heated, 300° oven for two hours.

Baked Steak with Onion Soup Mix

Ideal for tougher cuts of meat. Trim away fat
Lay steaks on foil. Sprinkle a package of dry onion soup mix over-all
Place generous pats of margarine or butter here and there on steaks; about one quarter pound in all for 2 pounds of steak.
Add 1 cup water.
Bring the foil over the steaks and seal on top.
Place in pre-heated 250° oven for two hours.
The onion soup mix may be saved and poured into a bowl and mixed with an equal amount of hot water–then used as a gravy or poured over the steaks.
This is also an excellent way to prepare steaks that have been in your freezer several months (even a year). But first trim away any freezer burn.

Ham on the Grill with Bar-B-Que Sauce

3/4" slices of ham: about 3/4 pound to the serving

Bar-b-Que Sauce for Ham (4 servings)

1 small can crushed pineapple
1/2 cup brown sugar
1/4 cup table mustard

Prepare the bar-b-que sauce by blending the crushed pineapple, brown sugar and mustard. You can do it with a spoon.
Since the ham is pre-cooked, it need only be broiled a few minutes on each side. Brush on the sauce after you have turned the slices over. In other words, use the sauce on the second side only.

Baked Chops in Wild Rice Stuffing

Use thick or "double chops." With wild game, trim away the fat.

Season the chops, then brown both sides. Prepare wild rice stuffing according to the recipe on page XXX.*

Place the stuffing in a baking dish or roaster.

"Submerge" the chops in the dressing.

Cover and place in a pre-heated 300° oven for 1-1/2 hours. Be sure the chops are tender and well done - all the way through.

*Most any stuffing (dressing) will work.

DESSERTS

Chocolate Chip Cookies

Ingredients:

1-1/2 cup chocolate chips
3-3/4 cup flour
3/4 cup sugar
1-1/2 cup brown sugar (compacted)
1/2 cup chopped nuts (of your choosing)
1-1/2 tsp. salt
1-1/2 tsp. soda
2 tsp. vanilla
3 eggs
3 sticks of butter or margarine

Using a blender, mix all ingredients except flour, nuts and chocolate chips. Now stir in these last three ingredients. Bake on a lightly greased cookie sheet in a pre-heated 350° oven for 10 to 12 minutes, depending on how soft or crisp you want the cookies.

Peanut Butter Cookies

Ingredients:

1 cup smooth peanut butter
2 cups flour
1 cup shortening (may substitute 1/2 margarine or butter)
1 cup sugar
1-1/4 cup brown sugar (packed)
3 eggs
1 tsp. soda
1 tsp. baking powder
1 tsp. vanilla
1/2 tsp. salt

Sift together flour, salt, soda and baking powder. Blend shortening and peanut butter until smooth. Beat together all ingredients, adding one egg at a time and the vanilla last. Drop 1 tbsp. of the dough at a time on a greased cookie sheet. Flatten with a fork, making criss-cross marks. Bake in a pre-heated 375° oven for 10 to 12 minutes.

Sugar Cookies

Ingredients:

4 cups flour
1 cup sugar
1 cup sour cream
1 cup shortening
1 tsp. soda
1/2 tsp. salt
1 tsp. vanilla
2 tsp. baking powder

Sift together the flour, baking powder, soda and salt. Blend the sugar into the shortening and combine with the dry ingredients. Next add the vanilla and sour cream. Refrigerate the dough for at least 30 minutes. Roll quite thin and cut in circles. Bake on a greased cookie sheet in a pre-heated 350° oven for 10 to 12 minutes. You may sprinkle a little additional sugar on top.

Molasses Cookies

Ingredients:

3 cups flour
1 cup molasses
1 cup brown sugar (compacted)
1 stick butter or margarine
3 eggs
1/2 cup boiling water
2 tbsp. soda
1 tbsp. cinnamon
1 tsp. allspice (ground)
1 tsp. ginger (ground)
1/2 tsp. salt

Sift together all dry ingredients, then add remaining ingredients. If the dough is not real workable, add more water or flour, whichever is needed. Roll thin; cut into desired shapes; bake on a greased cookie sheet in a pre-heated 375° oven for about 10 minutes.

Brownies

Ingredients:

4 squares of chocolate
2 cups sugar
1 cup shortening
1 cup flour
4 eggs
2 cups nuts, chopped (your choice)
2 tsp. vanilla

Melt the chocolate and combine with the shortening. Beat the eggs well. Combine all ingredients. Bake for 25-30 minutes in a square or rectangular pan in a pre-heated 375° oven.

Rhubarb Pie

Ingredients:

4 cups chopped rhubarb
1-1/2 cups sugar
3 eggs, beaten
1/4 cup flour
3/4 tsp. nutmeg
options - substitute 1 cup strawberries for 1 cup rhubarb

Using the same procedure as for any two-crusted pie, combine the dry ingredients; stir the beaten eggs in (thoroughly); stir in the rhubarb and place mixture–evenly–in the pie crust shell. Cover with top crust.

Ingredients for topping:

1/2 cup flour
1/2 cup sugar
1/2 cup butter

Combine the flour and sugar. Cut the butter into small pieces and stir into the dry mixture. Sprinkle topping over crust. Cover with foil and bake in a pre-heated 400° oven for 20 minutes. Remove foil and bake another 20 minutes or until crust is a golden brown.

Blueberry Pie

Ingredients:

3 cups cleaned berries, remove all unripe berries
1 cup sugar (rounded)
3 tbsp. flour
2 tbsp. butter, melted
dash of salt

Using the same procedure as for any two-crust pie, bake in a pre-heated 350° oven for 45 minutes. Sprinkle sugar over top crust.

Brown Betty

Ingredients:

3 cups chopped apples (peeled and cored)
1/2 cup brown sugar, (compacted)
2 cups bread crumbs
3 tbsp. butter, melted
4 tbsp. water
1 tsp. cinnamon

Stir the bread crumbs into the melted butter. Combine all ingredients and bake in a square or rectangular pan in a pre-heated 350° oven for 25 minutes.

Glorified Rice

Ingredients:

3 cups cooked rice
1 cup whipped cream, sweetened
1 can fruit cocktail, medium (#2)
1 small can crushed pineapple
1 small jar maraschino cherries
1 cup miniature marshmallows

Drain the cans and jar. Combine all ingredients and chill before serving.

Fruitcake

Ingredients:

1-1/2 cup dates, chopped
1-1/2 cup raisins
6 tbsp. butter
3 cups flour
2 cups boiling water
1 tbsp. cinnamon
1/2 tsp. cloves (ground)
1-1/2 cups chopped nuts (of your choosing)

1 small jar maraschino cherries
1 tsp. salt
2 cups sugar

Combine the raisins, dates, sugar, butter and water. Simmer for 20 minutes, stirring occasionally. Let cool. Add remaining ingredients. Bake in a loaf pan in a pre-heated 325° oven for 1-1/2 hours. May be stored, wrapped in foil and refrigerated or frozen.

Angel Food Dessert

Ingredients:

1 angel food cake
2 cups whipped cream (sweetened)
3 cups milk
4 egg yolks
1 cup sugar
2 tbsp. gelatin (unflavored)
4 egg whites, beaten
1/2 cup water
1 small jar maraschino cherries

Place the milk in a sauce pan. Stir in salt. Stir in the egg yolks, thoroughly. Add sugar and bring to a boil. Add the gelatin to the half-cup of water and stir into the milk-egg mixture. Let cool.
Stir in beaten egg whites. Let stand until the mixture begins to "set". Fold in the whipped cream. Cut or tear the angel food cake into small pieces. Layer the cake pieces on the bottom of a 9"x13" pan. Pour the liquid uniformly over the cake pieces. Cut up the cherries and scatter over the dessert.

Rice Krispie Bars

Ingredients:
5 cups Rice Krispies
4 cups miniature marshmallows
1/2 stick butter, melted
option: 1 cup peanut halves
Melt the butter and marshmallows together, stirring occasionally to blend. Remove from stove and add Rice Krispies. Stir until thoroughly coated. While still warm, press into a square pan. When cool, cut into squares.

Picnic and Cabin Cooking

Potato Salad with Dill

Ingredients to serve 6:

12 small new potatoes, sliced (with or without skins)
1 medium onion, peeled, sliced thin and broken into rings
4 tbsp. diced green sweet pepper
4 tbsp. diced red pepper
3 tbsp. chopped fresh dill
1/2 cup olive oil
3 tbsp. lemon juice or vinegar
1/2 cup sour cream
pepper to taste
garnish with paprika

Boil the potatoes in a covered saucepan for about 20 minutes or until done.
Gently combine all ingredients. Refrigerate at least 30 minutes before serving.

Baked Beans (doctored from the can)

Serving for 4:

1-#2-1/2 can (about 32 oz.) of pork and beans
2 pieces of thick bacon
1/2 cup brown sugar (or, 1/4 cup molasses and 1/4 cup brown sugar)
1/2 cup catsup
2 tbsp. mustard
a few pieces of green pepper
1 tbsp. chopped onion

Cut the bacon strips into half-inch pieces and fry over medium heat until light brown - not crisp. Place the pieces of bacon and a little of the grease in the bottom of a kettle. (Help the dishwashers by using the same kettle for frying the bacon as you will use for heating the beans.) Add the beans, brown sugar, catsup, mustard, onion, and green pepper. Stir and heat (medium). Bring to a slow boil, then simmer for at least fifteen minutes.....the longer the better. Stir occasionally.

The key ingredients are brown sugar and catsup - so if you are short any or all of the other additives, do not hesitate to "doctor" the beans with just these two items. Molasses may be substituted for all or part of the brown sugar.

Hamburgers

An old reliable - especially with the kids. Hamburgers always "hit the spot" when served with potato chips or French fries or potato salad.

Hamburger patties, fried slowly on both sides, are best served on traditional hamburger buns. Season with salt and pepper. They can be "doctored up" by adding a little chopped onion or one-half envelope of dried onion soup mix to each pound of hamburger.

If you have time, use the charcoal or gas grill - with barbecue sauce for seasoning - brushed on as the hamburgers broil (second side only).

Option: slices of sweet onion and/or tomatoes, sliced.

Hot Dogs (Wieners/Brats)

Boiled, or
Roasted over an open fire

They can be made extra-fancy by baking them in the oven (or over an open fire on a stick) with wrap-around strips of bread dough (from your grocer's dairy case).

For a HOT DOG SPECTACULAR, cut the wieners just over half way through - lengthwise. Place a strip of mild cheese or cheese spread in the incision. Now wrap a piece of half-fried bacon around the wiener, holding it in place with toothpicks. Place under the broiler or on the grill until the bacon is crisp and the cheese has melted. Serve with beans and/or potato salad.

Roasting Ears

Soak the ears of corn (husks and all) in water for at least 5 minutes. Wrap in foil and place in the embers of your camp fire (or use your gas or charcoal grill). Remove after an hour. Strip away husks and silk (use hot pads or "mitts"), serve with salt and butter.

If you use the grill, you need not wrap the corn in foil. Just soak them briefly in water and place them on the grill and turn every few minutes until the outside husks are singed.

Chili

Easy to fix - always a favorite - and it also makes a good "shore lunch." If used as a shore lunch, it will save valuable fishing or hunting time if you make it in advance and merely heat it over an open fire or on a portable gas stove.

4 generous servings:

1 pound hamburger

1 medium onion (chopped, but not fine)

2 small cans tomato soup

2 cans red kidney beans (or chili beans) - #2 size

1 can tomato sauce, Mexican style

Fry the hamburger (broken into small pieces) and the chopped onion together in an iron kettle or frying pan over medium heat. Be sure the bottom is first covered with a coat of oil. When the hamburger is brown, add the tomato soup, tomato sauce, seasonings and kidney beans. Let the chili come to a boil, then turn the heat down and let simmer for fifteen minutes or until piping hot.

Stew

A real favorite in camp and can be used as a shore lunch.

Since it takes so long to prepare a stew "from scratch," we are going to cheat a little! We will use canned beef stew as a base and a roast instead of regular stew meat. There just isn't enough meat in most canned stews to satisfy a hungry man.

4 servings:

2 cans of beef stew (24 oz. cans)

1 can mixed vegetables (#2 can)

1 can tomato soup

1 can tomato sauce

1-1/2 to 2 pounds of beef or wild game roast, cut into bite-size portions. (Leftover roast makes great stew meat)

If you don't happen to have leftover roast, prepare the roast at home to save time in camp. Use a cheaper cut. Prepare according to instructions on page 22. Medium doneness is best for stew meat.

Empty the contents of the cans of beef stew, mixed vegetables, tomato sauce and tomato soup into an iron kettle or deep iron skillet. Stir in pre-cooked meat chunks.

Simmer for 40 minutes; stir occasionally.

For a spicy stew, add catsup or Tabasco sauce to taste.

Logging Camp Cooking

Turn of the century lumberjacks worked hard and didn't make much money, but they were rewarded by generous portions of well prepared foods at every meal.

Sourdough Pancakes

Sourdough was used by the early settlers for both bread and pancakes. It would have been virtually impossible to prepare either without it under most pioneering conditions. The sourdough "starter" may be kept for long periods of time. Starter can be purchased in camping supply stores or gourmet shops.

Ingredients for 16-20 cakes:

1 cup starter
1 tbsp. sugar
1/3 tbsp. salt
2 cups water
2 cups flour

The night before, mix the ingredients together, thoroughly (except the starter). Add the starter and mix again. Let the mixture stand overnight in a warm room. The next morning, remove a cup of the starter (for next time) and place in a jar with a tight cover. Keep cool.
If the batter is too heavy you may have to stir in a little water to insure light, well-done cakes.

Parsnip, Rutabaga and Potato Soup

Ingredients to serve 8:

10 parsnips, scraped and sliced - about 1/4 inch
2 rutabagas, cubed - about 1/2 inch
4 large potatoes, peeled and cubed
3 carrots, sliced - about 1/4 inch
4 ribs celery, chopped (not in the original logging camp recipe)
1 large onion, peeled and chopped
1 pound stew meat, cut bite-size (or left-over roast)
2 tbsp. catsup
1/2 tsp. oregano

10 peppercorns
1/2 tsp. salt (or to taste)

In a soup pot, cover the beef and onion with water, bring to a boil, then reduce heat and simmer 1 hour.

Add all other ingredients, cover with as much water as it takes to make the soup the consistency you like. Bring to a boil, then reduce heat to simmer for another hour or until the meat and vegetables are tender.

Pot Roast

Trim fat from the beef roast.

Rub in salt and pepper--you may also want to try garlic salt.

Roll the roast in flour and brown all sides in cooking oil.

Add about one-half cup of water, cover tightly and cook slowly for two and one-half to three hours (275° to 300° oven). A "Dutch Oven" on top of the stove also works well.

For a true pot roast dinner, add whole small onions, carrots, and whole, peeled small potatoes the last hour. Be sure the vegetables are done before serving.

Baking Powder Biscuits

These biscuits go well with any meal but especially with a stew. In fact, the stew may be served over the biscuits.

2 cups flour
2 tbsp. (level) baking powder
1 tbsp. salt (level)
1 tbsp. sugar (level)
1/2 stick of butter or margarine (1/8 pound)
3/4 cup milk

Sift together the dry ingredients (flour, baking powder, salt and sugar). If you don't have a "sifter," shake them together (thoroughly) in a paper bag. Using your fingers, rub soft butter or margarine into the powdered ingredients until they are uniformly coated or sticky. Add the milk and work into a soft dough. Place the dough on waxed paper or a flour covered board. Pat it out until it is uniformly about 3/4 inch thick. Cut into squares (about two inches) or cut into circles - a cookie cutter or small cover will do. Reform the scraps and make these also into biscuits.

Arrange on a lightly greased cookie sheet (or use a pan) and bake in a pre-heated 400° oven for 10-12 minutes until they are well browned.

Part III

ETHNIC CONTRIBUTIONS TO MINNESOTA COOKING

Each new race or nationality which has come to Minnesota has brought along the best of its own cooking. The original Minnesotans, the Native Americans, knew how to enjoy the bounty of the lakes and woodlands and they shared this knowledge with the newcomers. Part III includes the best of the best of ethnic cooking.

The races and nationalities are listed in order, appropriately, according to the percent they make up of the state's population, with the exception of three groups of "newer Minnesotans" - the Asians, Hispanics and migrants from India. They are in a separate section.

These newer Minnesotans are having an amazing and disproportionate impact on the state. As we visit their restaurants we find an awful lot of Scandinavians, Germans and other of European descent eating these foods. It is good that we are learning to enjoy each other's traditions.

Scandinavian

Swedish Pancakes

Ingredients for about 18 cakes:

1 cup flour
3 cups milk
4 eggs
2 tbsp. sugar
pinch of salt

Thoroughly blend all ingredients in a mixing bowl. The batter should be quite thin. Spoon batter onto a hot griddle. Turn only once to prevent toughness.

Variations:

1) Pancakes are sometimes served with confectioners sugar on top and/or a great variety of syrups and berries.
2) Another variation is to make large, but thin, cakes and stack them 8

or 10 high with preserves between them. Cut and serve like a torte.
3) Bits of bacon or salt pork may be pre-fried and added to the batter.

Swedish Meatballs

Ingredients to serve 4:

1/2 pound ground beef
1/2 pound ground pork (or use all beef)
1/2 cup bread crumbs
1/2 cup cream (half and half will do)
1/2 cup water
2 tbsp. onion, chopped fine
1/2 tsp. salt
1/2 tsp. pepper
1 tsp. allspice
1 egg
butter for frying

Thoroughly blend the beef and pork, work in the seasonings, a little at a time for a thorough blend. Mix together the bread crumbs, cream and water and blend in. Beat the egg and work that into the mixture. Work into balls (small for hors d' oeuvres, large for a meal). Fry one first to check seasoning, then do the balance. Fry over moderate heat. Be sure they are done thoroughly.

Lutefisk

Use the fish from the market that is presoaked, but soak again for 3-4 hours before cooking. Put enough water in a kettle to completely cover the fish, but do not place the fish in the water until it comes to a rolling boil. Place the pieces of fish in a dish towel or cheesecloth and tie the ends together, like a purse. Submerge the fish in the boiling water. Water will cease boiling. When boiling resumes, remove fish. Beware of over-cooking which will make it like gelatin. Flake the fish away from the skin and bones into a serving dish. Serve with melted butter or a white sauce, usually over potatoes. Season with salt and pepper to taste. (See white sauce recipe below).

Baked:

Use fish that has been presoaked at the market. Soak for another 3-4 hours in cold water before cooking. Place skin-side down (or remove skin) in a buttered baking dish. Lightly season with salt and pepper. Bake in a medium oven (350°) for 40 minutes* or until done (the fish will flake easily with a fork). Flake the fish away from the skin and bones into a serving dish. Serve over potatoes with white sauce or melted butter. Season to taste.

White Sauce

2 tbsp. butter
2 tbsp. flour
1 cup milk (or cream)
a little salt and pepper
2 tbsp. lemon juice

Melt the butter–carefully; without burning–in a saucepan or double broiler. Add the flour and continue to cook for three minutes, stirring continuously. Stir in the lemon juice. Remove pan from the heat and slowly stir in the cup of milk. Return the pan to the stove and bring to a boil, stirring all the while. Place mixture in a double broiler, add salt and pepper, and cook until the sauce thickens. Beat with an egg beater.

Large fish may take up to 1 hour.

Norwegian

Torsk (creamed codfish)

Ingredients to serve 4 Scandinavians--6 normal people!

2 pounds codfish (half the weight if dried)
water

If dried fish is used, soak for 4 hours. Remove skin and bones. Boil in fresh water for 45 minutes. Cut fish into small pieces. Meanwhile, prepare a white sauce according to the recipe on previous page. Serve over potatoes. Season with salt and pepper to taste and top with a large pat of cold butter.

Potato Lefse*

Peel and boil as many potatoes as you need (figuring 1 medium potato for each lefse you plan to make). When potatoes are done, drain, and add a little milk and butter and mash well. For 8 to 10 - 14 inch lefses:

3 cups mashed potatoes
1 cup flour
1/4 cup heavy cream
1 tbsp. sugar

Mix together all ingredients (like pie crust). Form into 8 to 10 parts
and roll thin. Bake on lefse grill until brown; turn and bake the other
side.

*Courtesy Avis Sandeland, Clearbrook, MN

Finnish

Fruit Soup

Fruit soup may be served either at the start of the meal or as a dessert
or even for breakfast.

Ingredients to serve 8:

2 quarts water
1/2 cup raisins
1 cup prunes, sliced
1 cup apricots, sliced (or peaches or other fruit)
juice of 1/2 orange
juice of 1/2 lemon
1/2 cup sugar
1/2 cup tapioca
1/2 tsp. salt
1 stick cinnamon

Place the fruit in the water; bring to a boil and then reduce heat and
let simmer about 20 minutes. Let cool. Add all other ingredients and
cook until the tapioca is transparent. Serve hot or cold.

Finnish Soup (Moijakka)

Ingredients to serve 8:

2 pounds stew meat, cubed - bite-size
1 large onion, chopped

3 ribs celery, chopped

12 peppercorns

6 medium potatoes, peeled and chopped

1 medium rutabaga, chopped

1 medium head cabbage, shredded

6 carrots, sliced

1 turnip, chopped

1 beef bouillon cube dissolved in 1 cup water

1/2 tsp.

oil to brown meat

Brown the stew meat. Cover with water and simmer until meat starts to tenderize, about 30-40 minutes. Meanwhile, chop vegetables - not too small. Add celery, carrots, onion and peppercorns and let simmer another 30 minutes. Add all other ingredients except cabbage and cover with water. Simmer until potatoes, rutabaga and turnip pieces are tender. Add cabbage and simmer another 10 minutes.

Swedish Rye Bread (limpa)

Ingredients:

1 stick (1/2 cup) butter or margarine

1 cup brown sugar

1/2 cup molasses

2-1/4 cups boiling water

1 tsp. salt

2 pkg. dry yeast

1/2 tsp. sugar

1/4 cup warm (110°F) water

1 tbsp. anise seed

3 cups rye flour

3-4 cups white flour

Place butter, brown sugar and molasses in bowl. Pour boiling water over this mixture. Stir in salt.

Proof yeast with sugar and water until foamy.

Stir above mixture together. Add anise seed. Mix in flours. Dough will be sticky until it is completely kneaded. Knead until smooth and elastic. 15-20 minutes. Allow to rise in greased, covered bowl until double in bulk. Punch down and separate dough for loaves. Pat into greased pans; cover and allow to rise until nearly double in bulk. Will be soft to the touch; finger will leave impression. Bake at 350°F for 45 minutes. Brush with brown sugar syrup, (made by dissolving brown sugar in boiling water).

Danish Pastries

Basic recipe for pastry dough:

3 cups flour
1-1/4 cups milk
1 pkg. yeast (1-1/2 oz.)
3 tbsp. sugar
1/4 tsp. salt
1 egg
1/2 pound butter

Place yeast in mixing bowl. Beat the egg into the milk, add to the bowl along with salt and sugar. Stir in the flour until the dough becomes workable. Place dough on lightly floured board and knead thoroughly. Roll out the dough to about 1/3 inch thickness. Cut the butter into pats and place on half of the area of the sheet of dough. Fold the unbuttered half over the half with butter. Fold once more and then roll to original thickness. Fold again, twice, and roll again. If dough is too sticky or unworkable, refrigerate 15 minutes, then roll again. The dough should now be ready for making pastries of your design.

Fillings

Nut Filling

Chop or roll nuts of your choice until fine. To one-half cup of chopped nuts, add 3 tbsp. softened butter and 1/3 cup sugar. Blend thoroughly.

Vanilla Filling

1 cup milk
1 egg yolk
2 tbsp. flour
1 tbsp. sugar
2 tbsp. vanilla sugar

Mix together all ingredients except the vanilla sugar. Simmer about 5 minutes in a saucepan, stirring continuously. Let cool. Add vanilla sugar (stir in).

Preserves

Use your favorite jams or jellies.

Norwegian Crullers

Ingredients for about 3 dozen:

3 egg yolks
2 cups flour
4 tbsp. sugar
3 tbsp. cream
2 tbsp. butter, softened
1 tbsp. finely grated lemon or orange peel
optional: 2 tbsp. brandy or cognac

Mix together all ingredients, thoroughly, adding the flour last. Work into a dough; refrigerate 3 hours. Roll the dough into a thin sheet, no more than 1/4 inch. Cut the sheet of dough into strips about 3 inches long and 1/2 inch wide.
Make a slit in the middle of each piece (about 1 inch long). Pull one end of each strip through the slit. Cook in hot oil until crispy-brown. Sprinkle with sugar (regular or powdered).

Veal Roast with Dill Sauce

Ingredients to serve 6 to 8:
3-4 pound veal roast
salt and pepper
Lightly season the roast and place it in a roaster that has been well greased with butter. Bake in a medium oven for about one hour; do not over-roast. A meat thermometer is helpful. Meanwhile, prepare dill sauce as follows and serve over sliced roast.

2 tbsp. minced fresh dill or 1 tbsp. dry dill
1 tbsp. chopped onion
2 tbsp. butter
1 tbsp. flour
1 cup cream
salt and pepper to taste
Sauté the onion pieces until clear. Stir in flour and cook for 3 minutes. Stir in all other ingredients, seasoning to taste. Serve over sliced roast.

Rullepolse (Scandinavian meat roll)

Flank meat or other relatively thin "sheets" of meat that can be rolled are usually used. Meat scraps that would normally be used for stew meat (or hamburger) are also used (not tough pieces however). All meat should be boneless.

Lay the flank meat flat. Spread the scraps (bite-sized) evenly over the flank meat. Season lightly with salt and pepper. Sprinkle 1/3 tsp. ginger to each pound of meat. Chop a large onion and sprinkle over meat. Roll and wrap tightly with string.

Prepare a brine solution with enough water to cover the meat. Use enough salt to float an egg or a potato. Add 1/2 tsp. saltpeter per gallon of water. Boil until the salt dissolves.

When the brine has cooled, place the meat roll in non-metallic container and cover with the solution. Place a weight on top to keep the meat totally submerged. Let soak in cool place 48 hours. Remove and soak overnight in fresh water in a cool place.

Remove and place in fresh water again and boil slowly for two hours. Place meat in loaf pan; force to fit. Use more than one pan and cut meat to fit if necessary. Store in cool place with weight on top to hold shape.

Slice thin and serve cold.

Head Cheese

This tasty delicacy receives its name from the fact the pork used traditionally came from a hog's head. You may still use that source for this recipe, but hogs' heads may be a little hard to come by in your local market!

But here is an old favorite Scandinavian recipe.

2 pounds shank or beef roast
2 pounds pork shoulder roast or lean meat from a hog's head
10 allspice
5 bay leaves
1 tsp. garlic salt
1 tsp. white pepper
3 tbsp. brown sugar
2 onions, sliced (medium)
2 tbsp. salt

Chop both the beef and the pork into small pieces (about 1/2 bite-size).

Place in a crockpot and cover with water. Let simmer on low until very tender (about 4-5 hours).

Place the meat in a dishtowel; tie with a string; and place in a stone crock or other non-metallic container.

Make a spice-brine by adding the spices and brown sugar as listed above to enough water to cover the meat. Boil briefly, stirring continuously. Pour the solution over the meat.

Place a board on top of the meat and press down firmly. Place a clean rock on top of the board to maintain pressure.

Store in a cool place or under refrigeration. Wait a couple of days and then slice cold to serve--with vinegar on the side.

The Smorgasbord

The name "Smorgasbord" is used world-wide and applies to most any buffet featuring a variety of dishes. The original Swedish smorgasbord was more like an elaborate display of hors d'oeuvres, featuring among other things a variety of open-faced sandwiches, usually cut relatively small and in a variety of shapes. When eaten as a meal, it was customary to visit the table several times, choosing a few things each visit, perhaps beginning with herring, then moving to salads, smoked fish, sandwiches, cheeses, pickles, meatballs, sausages and eggs.

The recipes which follow are true to the original Swedish concept and most any of them, even by themselves, will serve as tasty hors d'oeuvres.

Sandwich Options

Use a variety of breads cut into different shapes and sizes. Leave them open-faced (no bread on top). Trim away the crust. Crisp breads and wafers are also appropriate.

Smoked Meats

Use thin slices of dried beef (Scandinavians often used smoked reindeer). Butter the bread. Add a layer of mayonnaise mixed with finely chopped hard-boiled eggs.* Top with the meat. Garnish with a little circle or dab of the mayonnaise-egg mixture on the meat.

Bring to a boil, turn off the heat and let sit 20 minutes or so for hard-cooked.

Shrimp

Use tiny, fresh-cooked shrimps. Stir together the shrimps and either red or white tartar sauce until the shrimps are well coated. Spoon a generous layer on the bread and top with two or three uncoated shrimps and perhaps a sprig of parsley.

Smoked Fish and Cream Cheese
(Smoked eel is a traditional favorite.)

Chop the smoked fish into tiny flakes. Stir together 3 parts cream cheese and one part mayonnaise. Thoroughly blend equal portions of the fish and cheese-mayonnaise, forming a spread. Garnish with a sprig of dill.

Herring and Potatoes

Use pickled herring and small boiled potatoes. Chop the herring quite fine. Slice the potatoes. Butter the bread. Add a leaf of lettuce and/or a little mayonnaise. Cover with sliced potatoes. Top with the herring.

Caviar

Most any variety of caviar (sturgeon, salmon, whitefish or cod) is appropriate. Use very small pieces of bread or use crackers. The caviar may be used by itself or with finely chopped hard boiled eggs or cold scrambled eggs. Butter the bread first.

Ham

Ham, of course, is good by itself, especially on dark breads; but for a different taste treat, add sliced prunes or raisins. A very thin spread of a gourmet mustard or mayonnaise may be used instead of (or with) butter.

Cheeses

Traditional smorgasbords feature a variety of cheeses by themselves, usually of the stronger varieties. Of course, cheese also makes a tasty sandwich. Milder cheese (such as Swiss or Cheddar) are better with bread. Butter the bread and then add a little mayonnaise and/or a piece of lettuce. Top with the cheese. Thinly sliced cucumbers and/or sliced radishes also go well with cheese sandwiches, also sliced green or ripe olives.

Salted* Herring

Flavor 1 cup of sour cream with 1 tbsp. dill seed (or 2 tbsp. chopped fresh dill and 1 tbsp. minced onion.) Cut the herring in pieces to fit the pieces of bread. Spread the sour cream mixture over the herring. Garnish with a sprig of dill.

Full Loaf Sandwich

This will make a spectacular centerpiece for your smorgasbord display. Use a whole loaf of unsliced bread. Place the loaf on end and make three or four cuts the full length of the loaf, thus making 4 or 5 slices of bread the length of the loaf. If you can slice the bread thinner without breaking the slices, you may try for even more slices! Now reconstruct the loaf but with a different filling on each slice. Any of the above may be used. When the loaf has been reconstructed, cover it completely (top and all 4 sides) with cream cheese, applied like icing on a cake. Garnish the loaf creatively. One possibility would be sliced green or ripe olives or sliced radishes.

To serve the gigantic sandwich, simply slice as you would a loaf of bread, being careful to hold it together (perhaps with a spatula) while transferring the slices to your guests' plates.

*Pickled herring may also be used

German

Black Rye Bread

Ingredients for 2 loaves:

3 cups flour, all-purpose
3 cups rye flour
1/2 cup molasses
2 pkgs. dry yeast
1 tbsp. caraway seeds (or cardamon)
2 cups water
2 tbsp. butter
2 tbsp. sugar
1 tsp. salt
1 cup unsweetened cocoa (optional - a modern day touch)

Mix together white flour, cocoa, yeast and seeds.

Meanwhile, heat together in a large kettle the molasses, water, salt, sugar and butter and heat until warm.

Combine the two mixtures and beat a slow speed 30 seconds and then 3 minutes at high speed (electric mixer).

Stir in the rye flour. Knead by hand about 5 minutes.

Cover and set in warm place about 30 minutes.

Punch down and divide, placing in two loaf pans. Make a few slashes in the tops of the loaves with a sharp knife. Cover and let stand in a warm place until the volume doubles (usually a little less than 1 hour).

Bake in a pre-heated 400° oven for about 30 minutes or until done.

Turn out of the pans and let cook on a rack.

Brush tops with butter or oil.

German Potato Salad

Ingredients to serve 8:

8-10 medium potatoes
10 slices lean bacon
3 ribs celery, chopped
1 medium to large sweet onion, sliced and rings broken up
1 cup vinegar
1/4 cup water
4 tbsp. flour
1/2 cup sugar
salt and pepper to taste
Fry and crumble the bacon.

If the potatoes are new, leave skins on; if not - peel. Cut potatoes in half and boil until done - but not mushy. Cut into bite-size cubes or slices.

While the potatoes are cooking, mix together in a saucepan all other ingredients except the salt and pepper. Bring to a boil and then reduce heat to simmer - stirring occasionally. When potatoes are done, drained and cubed, pour the liquid over the hot potatoes, add the bacon bits and season with salt and pepper as you gently stir them together. Serve hot.

Cabbage Strudel

Ingredients to serve about 16 one-inch servings:

3 cups cabbage, thinly sliced
1/2 cup onion, chopped

2 tbsp. butter, melted
4 tbsp. raisins
1 tsp. caraway seed
1 tsp. cardamon seeds
4 tbsp. chicken broth
1/2 tsp. salt
1/2 tsp. pepper, freshly ground
oil to sauté onion
6 sheets filo pastry, thawed out

Sauté the onion until clear. Add cabbage, both kinds of seeds and the chicken broth. Bring to a boil, then reduce heat and let simmer - covered - until cabbage is cooked. Stir in raisins, salt and pepper, being careful to distribute seasoning uniformly throughout. Arrange one piece of pastry sheet on a floured board or dish towel. Brush with melted butter. Lay another sheet on top and brush with butter; also a third sheet. Distribute half the mixture along the short side of the pastry sheets (about 1 inch from the edge). Roll tightly and place on cookie sheet. Brush with melted butter. Repeat with remaining pastry sheets and mixture. Bake in a medium oven about 20 minutes or until a golden brown. Cut into one-inch pieces to serve. Left over pieces may be refrigerated for a day or two, but warm before serving.

Goose with Sausage Stuffing

Ingredients to serve 8:

1 very large goose (12 pounds or larger: there is much waste in the carcass)
salt and pepper

Ingredients for the dressing:

2 cups celery, chopped
2 cups onion, chopped
4 cups croutons, pre-seasoned
2 cups sausage, crumbled
1 cup raisins
1 cup water chestnuts
1/2 pound melted butter or margarine
1 cup hot water
1/2 tsp. pepper
1/2 tsp. salt

1 tsp. poultry seasoning
oil or butter to sauté onion and celery

Clean the goose, inside and out. Remove visible fat. Season inside and out with salt and pepper. If the goose is very fat, parboil it for 30 minutes.

Prepare the stuffing. Sauté the onion and celery pieces. Brown the crumbled sausage. Melt the butter or margarine. Combine all the dry ingredients. Add the onion and celery, melted butter and hot water. Stir thoroughly.

Stuff the goose loosely. Place the balance of the stuffing in foil packages. Roast these packages separate from the goose.

Place the goose in a covered roaster and bake at 350° for one hour. Turn oven down to 275° and roast until the drumsticks and wings "wiggle" freely. (usually about 3 more hours)

The stuffing in the goose may be too fat to use; if so, discard it. If not too fat, mix thoroughly with stuffing baked separately.

Goose with Sauerkraut Stuffing

Use the previous recipe with stuff with 2 pounds of sauerkraut.

Sauerbraten

Ingredients to serve 8:

4 pound beef roast
enough butter or oil to brown roast

Marinade Ingredients:

2 cups red wine vinegar
1 large onion, chopped
3 stalks (ribs) celery, chopped
12 peppercorns
1 bay leaf
1 tsp. cloves
1 tsp. caraway seeds

Combine all marinade ingredients in a saucepan. Bring to a boil; reduce heat and let simmer about 5 minutes. Let cool. Place the roast in a covered container (glass or Tupperware) with the marinade poured over it. Marinate two days, turning whenever you think about it (2 or 3 times each day).

Remove the roast, pat dry, sprinkle with flour, and brown in oil. Save and strain the marinade, discarding solids. Pour marinade liquid over roast. Cover and cook over low heat until tender in a roaster or Dutch oven.

Marinade and juices from the roast may be used to make a gravy of your choice or may be served on the side and poured over servings of meat.

England/Scotland

Beef Tenderloin with Sherry Glaze

The English love their beef and here is a favorite for any special occasion.

Ingredients for 8 servings:

5 pounds beef tenderloin - all fat removed
1 pound fresh mushrooms (of your choosing)
2 pounds baby carrots
3 pounds small potatoes, preferably new
1/4 cup sherry (preferably cooking sherry)
2 tbsp. cooking oil
1 tsp. lemon pepper
1 tsp. thyme
1 tsp. rosemary
1 tbsp. lemon juice
salt to taste

Sauté the mushrooms in the vegetable oil until they curl.
Pre-cook the potatoes (skins on if new) and carrots in boiling water about 10 minutes. Do not over-cook. Should be able to pierce with fork but with difficulty.
Place loin on an oiled rack in a roasting pan. Tuck under the smaller end of the loin if necessary for even thickness. Sprinkle the seasonings (including lemon juice) evenly over the loin. Brush on the sherry (and brush again every 10 minutes).
Bake at 400° for 20 minutes and another 10 minutes at 350°.
Place mushrooms, carrots and potatoes around the loin. Brush the vegetables with the sherry. Bake another 10 or 15 minutes or until the vegetables are tender. If you are using a meat thermometer - until 140° for rare or 160° medium.

Serve on a platter with vegetables surrounding the loin and the mushrooms on top of the meat.

Some guests will probably request horseradish.

Horseradish Slaw

Great with all that beef the British eat! Serve as vegetable salad.
Ingredients for 8 servings:

6 cups cabbage, sliced thin and then chopped
4 medium beets (may use canned)
1/2 pound small sweet peas
1/2 cup yogurt, plain
1/2 cup sour cream
3 tbsp. prepared horseradish

Clean, trim and boil the beets in water until tender. (If large, cut them in half). It will take about 30 minutes. Let cool and chop fairly fine.

Steam the peas until tender; let cool.

Combine the cabbage, beets and peas and refrigerate until chilled.

Thoroughly blend the sour cream, yogurt and the horseradish.

Stir together the vegetables and the dressing.

Serve on a lettuce leaf.

Lamb Chops with Mint

A favorite in Scotland
Ingredients for 4 servings:

8 loin chops, thick cuts

Marinade ingredients:

3 lemons, juice of
1/3 cup fresh mint (if not available, try mint jelly)
3 tbsp. honey
1 tbsp. garlic, minced
1 tbsp. cornstarch

Combine all ingredients except the cornstarch. Generously coat meat and marinate, refrigerated in a shallow dish about 3 hours. Turn and coat every hour. Remove meat. Combine the cornstarch with the marinade. Add to a saucepan and bring to a boil. Reduce heat and let cook until it thickens (only a minute or two).

Brush the marinade on both sides of the chops.

Broil the chops on an oiled grill about 6 inches from the heat (hot coals or broiler on high). Turn after 5 minutes. Another 4 or 5 minutes should do it. Check for desired doneness.

Game Birds in Sherry Cream Sauce

Although created for wild game, this recipe works well with domestic fowl.

Ingredients for 4 servings:

2 grouse (or larger birds)
1/2 cup sherry (preferably cooking sherry)
1 pint heavy cream (unless you are diet conscious)
4 tbsp. vegetable oil
salt and pepper to taste
1 cup water

Skin and disjoint the birds into quarters plus the wings*. Brown in vegetable oil in a heavy skillet (preferably iron) over medium heat. Brown lightly, do not let burn.

Add water, reduce heat, cover and let simmer one hour or until tender, turning occasionally.

Remove cover; cook off remaining liquid (but do not let burn). Reduce heat. Add cream; stir in sherry; allow to thicken slightly. Add salt and pepper to taste.

Small birds should be prepared whole or cut in half

Fowl Basted with Apple Sauce

Ingredients for 4 generous servings:

2 chickens or pheasants, split and skin removed
1 cup apple sauce (canned will do)
1/2 tsp. sage
1/2 tbsp. poultry seasoning
dash salt
2 tbsp. apple cider (or vinegar)

Place the halved fowl cavity side down on a greased rack in a roasting pan. Bake in a pre-heated medium oven (325° 0 350° degrees) for 30 minutes.

Meanwhile, blend seasonings into apple sauce. Brush liberally over birds (at end of 30 minutes). Bake another 20 minutes and baste again. Bake another 15 minutes and brush on once more. If birds are still not tender, return to heat until done.

Stuffed Goose (Chestnut and Sausage Stuffing)

Ingredients:

1 large goose
salt and pepper

Clean bird inside and out. Remove fat. If the bird is very fat or if it is suspected to be an older bird, parboil in water one hour.
Rub with salt and pepper inside and out.

Ingredients for Chestnut and Sausage Stuffing

2-1/2 cups of croutons or cubed stale bread
1 cup roasted, shelled chestnuts, coarsely chopped
1 pound seasoned pork sausage, fried and crumbled
1 tbsp. garlic, minced
1/4 pound butter or margarine, melted
1 cup hot water
2 cups mushrooms pieces (your favorite)
1 large onion, chopped
1 stalk celery, chopped
2 tsp. poultry seasoning
1/2 tsp. savory
1/2 tsp. salt
4 tbsp. brandy
1/2 tbsp. white pepper, freshly ground
2 tbsp. vegetable oil

If roasted chestnuts are not available, boil them in water for about 10 minutes. Peel them while warm.
Sauté the onions, celery, garlic, mushrooms and chestnuts in vegetable oil until onion is translucent and nuts start to crispen. Do not let burn.
Remove the ingredients to a bowl. Using the same skillet and oil,

brown the pork sausage. Crumble the sausage with a spatula as it browns. Remove and add to the bowl of onions, celery, garlic, mushrooms and nuts.

Melt the butter in the same skillet. When it is melted, add the cup of hot water. Stir together.

Meanwhile, add all remaining ingredients (croutons, seasonings and brandy) to the bowl. Stir together very well. Add butter-water mixture and stir again, mixing thoroughly.

When you are ready to roast the bird (not before) stuff loosely. Place the remainder of the stuffing in foil, seal and bake alongside the goose.

Roast the goose in a covered roaster, preferably on a rack to keep it out of the grease - in a medium-hot oven for one hour, then reduce heat to medium. An 8 pound goose will take about 3 hours, but start checking after 2-1/2 hours for desired doneness and tenderness. Drumsticks should move easily when done.

Irish

Corned Beef and Cabbage

Ingredients for 6:

3 pounds corned beef
3 carrots, chunked
3 onions (fairly large), chopped
1 large head cabbage
1 tbsp. dry mustard
1 tbsp. fresh thyme, chopped
1 tsp. salt
2 tsp. freshly ground black pepper

Place the corned beef, vegetables and seasonings (except the cabbage) in a soup pot. Cover with water. Bring to a boil, reduce heat and let simmer for an hour.

Quarter the cabbage and add to the pot. Add more water if necessary to cover. Let simmer about another hour and a half until meat and other ingredients are tender.

Serve on a platter with corned beef sliced. Serve with potatoes. Use prepared mustard seasoning.

Irish Stew

Ingredients for 6 servings:

2 pounds lean lamb or veal, cubed (about 1/2 inch). You may add a couple of sprigs of dill to the stew while cooking
3 tbsp. vegetable oil
2 onions, separated into rings
3 carrots, chunked (thick slices)
1 parsnip or turnip if available, sliced
6 cups beef broth
8 medium potatoes, quartered
2 tbsp. celery, chopped
salt and pepper to taste
chives or parsley for garnish

Brown the veal along with the onions and celery in the oil in the cooking pot.
Add all other ingredients (with a dash of salt and pepper) - except garnishment. Bring to a boil then reduce heat to simmer. Let cook about 2 hours our until meat and vegetables are tender. You may have to add water from time to time.
Add salt and pepper to taste before serving. Garnish with chopped chives or parsley.

Split Pea Soup

Ingredients to serve 6:
1-1/2 cups split peas (cleaned, picked through and rinsed)
1 ham hock or 1 cup diced, pre-cooked ham
5 cups chicken broth
1 onion, chopped
2 tbsp. cooking oil (traditionally bacon drippings)
2 stalks celery, chopped fine
2 potatoes, peeled and diced
1 carrot, diced
1 tbsp. flour
3 bay leaves
1/2 tsp. savory
1/4 tsp. ground cloves
salt and freshly ground pepper to taste
parsley flakes to garnish (or chopped fresh)

Sauté the onion, celery and garlic in oil in a skillet. (Do not burn). Add flour

and stir in, continuing cooking only about a minute. Add a cup of the broth and stir until flour is dissolved, smoothly.

Transfer skillet ingredients to a soup kettle. Add all other ingredients (except the parsley, salt and pepper) and bring to a boil. Reduce heat to simmer and cook (bubbly) for 40 minutes, stirring occasionally.

Add salt and pepper to taste.

Pour into bowls and garnish with parsley.

Polish

Filled Dumplings (Pierogi)*

2 cups flour
1/2 cup milk
1 whole egg and 1 egg yolk
2 tbsp. sour cream
1/2 tsp. salt
2 tbsp. butter

Mix ingredients and knead to a soft pliable dough. Let rest for 10 minutes covered in a warm place. Divide dough in halves and roll thin, cut circles with large biscuit cutter. Place a small spoonful of filling a little to one side. Moisten edges with water, fold over and press edges together firmly. Be sure they are well sealed to prevent the filling from running out. Drop Pierogi into salted boiling water. Cook gently for 5 minutes. Lift out of water gently with perforated spoon and serve with melted butter.

Fillings for Pierogi

Cheese and Potatoes:

1 heaping cup mashed potatoes
1 small cup dry cottage cheese
salt and pepper to taste
few chives or onion, cut fine

Mix thoroughly, but lightly and fill. Serve with melted butter.

Cottage Cheese:

1 cup cottage cheese
1 tsp. melted butter
1 egg, beaten
3 tbsp. sugar
3 tbsp. currants
1 tsp. lemon juice

Cream cheese with melted butter. Add other ingredients and mix well. Fill Pierogi. Serve with melted butter and sour cream.

Prune Filling:

1 cup cooked prunes
1 tbsp. sugar
1 tsp. lemon juice

Soak prunes overnight in water. Cook with sugar and lemon juice. When cool remove stones from prunes and fill Perogi. Serve with melted butter or whipping cream.

Fish Soup (Zupa z Ryby)*

Use as many different kinds of fresh fish as are available. Wash and clean fish (use all those too small for other use). Place fish in a large kettle. Cover with water, salt and pepper to taste. Add 1 onion, 2 bay leaves, about 6 peppercorns or wholespice. Celery and carrots also can be used for flavor. Bring to a boil. Add 1 cup cold water, do this 3 times as it keeps the fish firm. Then cook slowly for an hour or so. Either drain or carefully remove fish from broth. To about 1 cup of sour cream add a small amount of the hot broth into the sour cream slowly. When broth and cream are blended put back on fire to heat. Add more pepper for flavor. To serve pour soup over boiled potato or serve a bowl of potatoes if desired.
NOTE: We have used large fish heads, fins and back bones from fresh fish. Then just drain the broth to use as soup. This is a very good old Polish recipe for people who live near a lake and have fresh fish available.

Duck Soup (Czarnina)*

Cut up in pieces 1 duck and boil with 1 onion, 2 carrots, 4 ribs of celery, allspice, a bay leaf, and 1 tsp. marjoram for 1 hour. Then add 1 cup raisins, 30 prunes, 1 apple cut up in pieces. When fruits and meat and vegetables are done, mix 1 cup duck blood with 2 tbsp. flour and 2 tbsp. vinegar. Add to the soup and let cook slowly 1/2 hour. The blood should be diluted with vinegar to keep it from setting. Serve with potato dumplings boiled separately.

Potato Dumplings:

Grate 4 or 5 large potatoes, pour off the accumulated water and add 1/2 cup flour, a pinch of baking powder and a tbsp. salt and boil in salted water. (Drop 1/2 tsp. dough at a time into the boiling water to form dumplings.) Drain in cold water and serve separately. Don't add them to the boiling soup, just in your soup dish.

*Courtesy Kay Bargen, Deerwood, MN

Italian

Brushetta (Party Toast)

Ingredients for 8 slices of Italian bread, (similar to French bread) cut diagonally into half-inch thick slices:

2 tomatoes, chopped
6 green onions, chopped (use white parts only)
1 cup black olives, pitted and sliced
1 tbsp. capers
1 tbsp. minced garlic
3 tbsp. olive oil (in 3 parts)
2 tbsp. lemon juice
1 tbsp. chopped fresh oregano or basil or parsley
2/3 cup grated parmesan cheese

Make a paste by combining the blending the olives, 1 tbsp. olive oil, capers, lemon juice and garlic.
Combine chopped tomatoes, onion, herbs and 1 tbsp. olive oil (use a spoon).
Brush both sides of bread slices with olive oil and toast in a 400° oven.

Spread the paste on each slice of toast. Top with tomato mixture.
Sprinkle with a little parmesan.
Return to oven just long enough for the cheese to melt.

Fettuccine Alfredo with Mushrooms

Intended as a first course.
Ingredients to serve 8:

1 pound Fettuccine
1-1/2 cups mushrooms, sliced (preferably morels)
3 tbsp. cognac
1-1/2 cups cream (traditionally heavy)
6 tbsp. butter, melted
1/3 cup grated parmesan cheese
1/2 tsp. salt
1/2 tsp. pepper
water to cook Fettuccine

Combine 2 tbsp. of the melted butter, cognac, cream, salt and pepper.
Bring to a boil; reduce heat to simmer; add mushrooms; cook 10
minutes or until the mushrooms are tender.
Meanwhile, cook the Fettuccine in a pot of boiling water for about 3 or
4 minutes or until tender. Drain. Toss with the remaining melted
butter. Add creamed mushroom mixture and toss.
Serve with grated parmesan.

Anchovy Salad

Ingredients for 8 servings:

8 anchovy fillets
1/2 cup sliced black olives
1 head cauliflower
1/3 cup olive oil
1 tbsp. vinegar (preferably white wine)
3 tbsp. minced marjoram (or other favorite herb)
1/3 cup capers
1 cup pickled red peppers, sliced
water to cover cauliflower plus 1 tsp. salt for the water

Break the cauliflower head into smaller pieces. Cover with water (salted) and bring to a boil; reduce heat and cook for about 4 minutes until cauliflower is tender but still crisp. Drain and let dry.

Toss with all other ingredients. Refrigerate (up to 3 days).

Seafood Soup

Ingredients for 8 servings:

2 pounds mussels or scallops or boneless fish or combinations thereof
1 large can (32 oz.) plum tomatoes, chopped (save juice)
1 large onion, broken into rings
3 tbsp. minced garlic
4 cups water
2 cups white wine
3 tbsp. chopped oregano
1/2 tsp. Tabasco or other hot sauce
2 tbsp. olive oil
1 cup parsley, fresh, chopped

If you use mussels, clean, de-beard and cook in boiling water until they open.

Sauté the onion rings in the oil until translucent; do not burn.

Combine the following in a large soup kettle; water, wine, seafood, tomatoes, tomato liquid from the can, garlic, oregano and Tabasco.

Bring to a boil and then reduce heat and simmer 15 minutes or until the seafood is done.

Serve with garlic toast.

African American

Creamy Peanut Soup

Ingredients for 6 servings:
2 tbsp. oil
1/2 cup chopped celery (fine)
1 large onion, chopped fine
6 cups chicken broth
1-1/2 cups peanut butter (creamy style)
2 cups cream
salt and pepper to taste

Sauté the onion and celery in the oil. Combine with the broth in a large saucepan. Bring to a boil, then reduce heat to simmer. Add peanut butter and stir until blended. Add salt and pepper. Strain out solids and discard. Add cream, slowly, stirring it in. Stir over low heat for 2 or 3 minutes but do not let boil.

Tabboulah

Serve as a side dish or salad.
Ingredients for 6 servings:

1 cup wheat (traditionally bulgur)
1/2 pound Tofu, minced
3 tomatoes, sliced
1 cup black olives, pitted and sliced
1 lemon (juice of)
2 tbsp. olive oil
salt and pepper to taste
parsley flakes to garnish
lettuce leaves
2 cups water

Heat the water to boiling and pour over tofu. Let sit one hour, drain. Toss together all ingredients. Serve on lettuce leaves, garnished with parsley.

Harira (Stew)

Ingredients to serve 8:

1-1/2 pounds tender cut of lean beef
4 tbsp. olive oil
1 large onion, chopped
3 ribs celery, chopped
12 peppercorns
1/3 cup cilantro, chopped fine
1 tsp. ginger, grated or ground
1 stick cinnamon
2 quarts beef broth (chicken may be substituted)
2 quarts water
1-1/2 cups chickpeas (may substitute white beans)
6 medium tomatoes, sliced

1 cup lentils

3 tbsp. flour (to thicken)

salt to taste

1/4 cup parsley, chopped, for garnish

Soak chickpeas.

Cut beef into bite-size cubes. Place oil in heavy skillet; brown beef, celery and chopped onions simultaneously. Add beef broth, peppercorns, cilantro, ginger and cinnamon stick. Bring to a boil, reduce heat, and simmer, covered at least one hour our until meat is tender.

Meanwhile, in a saucepan, pour two quarts of water and add the drained chickpeas and a little salt. Bring to a boil, then reduce to simmer - for at least one hour or until the beans are soft. When chickpeas are tender, add lentils and continue cooking until they are tender (15-20 minutes).

When the meat is tender, add the diced tomatoes to the skillet. (For more of a tomato taste, add 1/2 cup catsup or 3 tbsp. tomato paste). Continue cooking another 15 minutes. Be sure meat is tender. At this point, remove and discard cinnamon stick.

Combine the contents of the skillet and the kettle, stirring thoroughly together. Continue to simmer. Add the flour, one tbsp. at a time, thoroughly stirring in the flour each time before adding the next spoon. Continue simmering and stirring until the stew is quite thick. Taste for seasoning. Add more salt and pepper if necessary. Serve in bowls garnished with parsley.

Shrimp and Chicken with Rice

Ingredients for 6 servings:

1 large chicken

36 medium shrimp (cleaned but not shelled)

2 large onions, chopped

1 large green (bell) pepper, seeded and sliced

3 tomatoes, quartered

2 cups mixed vegetables (may include sliced carrots, cut green beans, peas, celery, broccoli or cauliflower)

2 cups rice

1 tsp. salt (level)

1 tsp. pepper, heaping

1/2 small can tomato paste

Feel free to add other favorite spices, but taste as you go

flour (to coat chicken before frying)

vegetable oil to sauté onion and brown chicken

Cut up the chicken, disjointing the drumsticks from the thighs and the wings from the breasts. Cut the breasts into a total of 6 pieces. Remove skin.

Sauté the onion and pepper strips in 2 tbsp. vegetable oil; use a large kettle, preferably iron. Remove onion and pepper and set aside. Add 1 tbsp. vegetable oil to the pot; dredge the chicken pieces in flour, and brown - turning pieces until pink disappears on all sides.

Meanwhile, steam or boil the vegetables in a separate kettle until tender but still crisp. Do not over-cook.

Also in a separate kettle, boil the shrimp until they turn white (opaque).

Combine all ingredients in the large iron kettle. Add enough water to cover the chicken parts and other ingredients, barely. Bring to a boil and then reduce to simmer. Add rice and tomato paste. Cook over low-medium heat (just bubbly), not boiling) until chicken is tender (20-30 minutes). If it becomes too thick, add water. (The consistency should be like a thick soup.)

Stove Top Chicken

Ingredients for 8 servings:

8 quarters chicken
1 large onion separated into rings
1 can tomato paste
4 tbsp. peanut butter
8 eggs, hard boiled, shelled and sliced
12 whole peppercorns
3 tsp. salt
1 tbsp. garlic, chopped fine
2 tsp. cumin seeds
1 tsp. oregano
enough water to cover chicken pieces
2 tbsp. vegetable oil to sauté onion rings

Sauté onion rings in a large kettle (preferably iron) until translucent (about 2 minutes). Add 1 cup of water, the peanut butter and the tomato paste. Stir together. Mix in the spices. Add the chicken quarters (skin on or off as you please). Add enough water to cover the chicken. Cook over medium heat for 40 minutes. (do not let boil - more of a simmer, but bubbly). Add egg slices. Cook another 10 minutes or until the chicken is tender.

Serve with rice.

Native American

Wild Rice Stew (Ojibwe)

1 cup wild rice
2 pounds stew meat
1 onion, chopped
1 cup celery, chopped
1 can cream of mushroom soup
1/2 cup green pepper, chopped
1/8 pound butter
1 can mushrooms (4 oz.)

Prepare the wild rice by simmering in water until kernels flower out.
Cut meat into bite-size pieces. Brown in a hot skillet.
Sauté onion, celery and green pepper in butter over low heat until onions are clear (three or four minutes).
Use a greased, covered baking dish. Place all ingredients in the baking dish and mix well. Cover and bake two hours in medium oven (350°).
Add water if necessary to prevent dryness.

Pumpkin and Squash (Dakota Sioux and Ojibwe)

Both were Native American foods and found wherever Indians chose to raise gardens. Early explorers brought the seeds from these plants back to Europe.

Indian cooks use at least three methods of preparation:

Method #1:

Cut into chunks.
Leave skin on.
Scrape off seeds and "stringy" particles.
Bake by the fire or on the grill, turning for even cooking.

Method #2:

Remove the skin and the seeds.
Cut into small pieces; place in pot.

Add a little water and maple sugar.
Cook over low heat until soft enough to be mashed.

Method #3:

Cut off top (much as a child does when making a jack-o-lantern).
Remove seeds.
Stuff with pre-cooked wild rice.
Add a little water to keep moist.
Place top back on.
Bake with low heat.

Maize (corn - Dakota Sioux)

Corn is native to this continent and is another food explorers brought
back to Europe. Originally in warmer climates, it is believed it was
brought north to the Upper Midwest by the Sioux, Indian corn required
a longer growing season than today's varieties and it was difficult to
raise in colder climates. For the Indians of the plains, it was the main
staple food, much as wild rice was for the Woodland Indians. Originally
corn was prepared in essentially six ways:

Method #1:

Cut the kernels from the cob and cook with a little water and
appropriate seasoning (such as sage).

Method #2:

Roasting: Remove the silk. Rewrap the husks around the ear. Soak in
water until thoroughly saturated. Roast in coals until corn is cooked
through by the steam.

Method #3:

Corn Bread. Let corn dry on the cob. Scrape kernels from the cob.
Grind or pound. (originally was done between stones) until it becomes
a coarse flour. Add water gradually to make a dough. Bake on a flat
rock by the fire. Some tribes made ovens (southwest).
Sometimes a little lye water was added as the dough was made. Lye
was made by boiling the ashes from hardwoods. The solution was
allowed to cool. The ashes would settle out and were strained through
a sieve made of willows or rushes.

Method #4:

Succotash. Corn and other vegetables (try beans) are boiled together with a little fat added for flavor (a sweetening effect). Use just enough water to cover.

Method #5:

Dried corn soup. Corn is allowed to dry on the cob. It is then scraped off and boiled in water. Approximately three cups of water should be used for every cup of corn. Indians used a variety of seasonings, but animal fat was often added to enhance the flavor.

Method #6:

Parched. Dried corn is scraped from the cob and cooked in a hot, covered container. It must be stirred constantly for about ten minutes.

Rabbit or Gray Squirrel (Ojibwe)

2 snowshoe or cottontail rabbits or 4 gray squirrels

1/2 cup cooking oil

1 cup cooking wine

2 onions, sliced

1 tbsp. allspice

1 tsp. salt, a couple of dashes of pepper

1/4 cup flour

2 tbsp. sugar

Cut the rabbits into pieces as you would a chicken. Make a marinade of the oil, wine, onions, allspice, salt and pepper. Cover meat; cover dish; refrigerate and marinate for two days. Drain on paper towels, but save marinade.

Dredge meat in seasoned flour and brown in cooking oil. Remove meat and pour off all oil and fats. Return meat to pan and cover with marinade, adding sugar. Bring to a boil, then reduce heat and simmer until tender (about 45 minutes to 1 hour).

Pickled Tongue (Ojibwe)

For 4 to 6 deer tongues:

1 pint vinegar

1 pint water

2 tbsp. sugar

1 tsp. whole cloves

1 tsp. whole allspice

1 tsp. whole black peppers
1/2 tsp. mustard seed
1/2 tsp. salt

Wash tongues in salted water. Place in fresh water. Add one tbsp. allspice and let simmer one to two hours or until tender. (It will never get really tender). Let cool and peel off skin and cut off root ends. Place in jars and submerge in a pickling solution prepared from the above ingredients which has been boiled for about 10 minutes.
Refrigerate and let stand one week before eating.

Heart (Ojibwe)

The heart from any big game animal was a favorite of early Native Americans. It was broiled whole, sliced and fried, or cut into chunks and added to stews or soups.
Here's a modern day Indian recipe for stuffed heart you may like to try:

Clean the heart, cut open and remove arteries, veins and fat.
Prepare stuffing of two cups of dried bread pieces, 1/4 cup chopped celery, 1/4 cup chopped onion and seasoned to taste with salt and pepper. Add generous pats of butter as you stir the mixture together.
Stuff heart and close opening with skewers. Season outside of heart with salt and pepper. Roll in flour, and brown in cooking oil.
Bake in medium oven (325°) for 1-1/2 hours. Slice and serve with stuffing. (Extra stuffing may be baked in foil alongside the heart).

Poached Whitefish (Ojibwe)

The fish is first cleaned (gutted and scaled) and then cut into chunks or strips about two inches wide. You may prefer to filet the fish and remove the skin.
The fish chunks are placed in a container of cold water. Favorite seasonings were added. You may wish to add a few whole, black peppers, salt and a bay leaf or two. A favorite with present day Indian people is to add a chunk of salt pork.
The water is brought to a boil and then removed far enough from the coals to just simmer. When the fish flakes easily (about 10 minutes after coming to a boil), remove and serve.
Bite-size pieces dipped in melted butter are the equal of lobster.

Czechoslovakian

Kolaches

If there was ever a national confectionery, it is the kolache, a natural part of any celebration or holiday.

Ingredients for 4 dozen:

6 cups flour, all-purpose
1-1/2 cups milk, lukewarm
2 eggs
1/2 cup vegetable oil
2 envelopes dry yeast, dissolved
1 tsp. salt
vegetable oil to brush pastry

Ingredients for fillings:
Try your favorite fillings. Possibilities include prunes, apricot, poppy seed, applesauce or jams of various kinds. Cottage cheese is another option.

Start with half the flour - add the eggs, milk, salt and oil. Mix well until dough is smooth. Add dissolved yeast and as much of the remaining flour as it takes to make the dough easy to handle (not sticky).

Place dough on a floured surface and knead until smooth (8 to 10 minutes).

Put in a large greased bowl. Bring greased side up. Cover with dish towel.

Place somewhere warm (over 80°) and let rise until size doubles.

Punch down dough and divide into two portions. Cover one half. Cut off small chunks of dough about the size of a large walnut. Make them ball-shaped. Place the balls on a greased cookie sheet (about 12 to a sheet). Using your fingers, flatten the center of each ball, leaving a half-inch rim around the edges of the circle. Fill the center with filling (about 1 tbsp.). Form and fill 2 kolaches, then form and fill 2 more, then 2 more, etc.

Bake at 400° for about 10 minutes or until a light brown. Let cool on wire racks.

Repeat the process with the second half of the dough.

Jewish

Potato Latkes #1

Ingredients for about 24 potato pancakes:

4 medium potatoes, grated (russets work well)
1 medium onion, chopped fine
3 tbsp. matzo meal (you may substitute all purpose flour)
1 egg, beaten
1/2 tsp. salt
1/2 tsp. pepper
oil

Combine all of the ingredients in a bowl. Place a generous amount of oil (about 1/2 inch) in a skillet and heat (medium). When it is hot, drop one tbsp. of the mixture into the oil. It will tend to flatten out. If the mixture does not hold together, add a little milk to the mixture. Cook until a golden brown, turning once. This should take about 3 minutes.

Serve with any of the following: smoked fish, caviar, applesauce, sour cream or yogurt.

Potato Latkes #2 (with apple)

Ingredients for about 1 dozen pancakes: (a slightly different recipe)

2 cups grated or finely chopped potatoes
1 cup grated or finely chopped apple (no peel or core)
4 tbsp. flour
1 egg
1/4 tsp. salt
1/2 tsp. pepper
oil for frying

Combine apple and potato; add and stir in all other ingredients. Pre-heat a generous amount of oil (about 1/2 inch) in a heavy skillet so that the oil is ready when you finish mixing the batter. Using a tablespoon, drop 3 spoonfuls per pancake into the hot oil. Allow about 3 minutes to brown on bottom side, then turn with a spatula; fry until brown on both sides. If the batter is so thick that is does not flatten out on its own when dropped in the oil, gently flatten with a spatula. Option: sprinkle with confectionery sugar.

Matzo Balls (Served in Soups)

Ingredients for 12 balls:

1/2 cup matzo meal
4 eggs
1 tbsp. cooking oil (traditionally chicken fat)
1 tsp. minced onion
2 tbsp. chopped parsley
3 quarts water
just a dash of salt and pepper

Beat eggs and stir in meal, oil (or fat), onion and parsley. Cover and refrigerate 1 hour.
Using a large kettle (allowing for balls to expand as they cook), bring water to a boil.
Meanwhile, wet hands and then form the dough into balls the size of walnuts. Drop into boiling water. After about 5 minutes, the balls will be noticeable larger. Remove with slotted spoon and serve in hot soup. Soup can be of any type but is most often chicken.

Welsh

Rarebit

Ingredients for 4 servings:

8 oz. cheddar cheese (or that of your liking), grated
2 eggs, beaten
2 tbsp. prepared mustard
1/4 cup cream (traditionally heavy)
1 tbsp. Worcestershire sauce
1/8 tsp. pepper (cayenne preferred)
4 slices toast, cut diagonally

Thoroughly mix together all ingredients with a spoon (except the toast).
Spread out the toast on a grill or a broiling pan. Spoon the cheese mixture over the toast. Broil until the surface bubbles and starts to turn brown. (do not burn).

Potato Soup

Ingredients for 6 servings:

4 medium potatoes, peeled and cut into 1/2 inch cubes
1 large onion, chopped coarse
1 cup green onions, chopped (use white portion only but save greens)
3 tbsp. celery, chopped
1 cup milk
2 tbsp. vegetable oil
salt and pepper to taste
5 cups water to boil potatoes

Boil the potatoes in salted water until soft.
Sauté the celery, onion and white portion of green onions in oil until onion is translucent.
Puree the potatoes and water (in small batches) in a blender.
Place all contents back in the soup kettle and simmer for 5 minutes, stirring.
Stir in milk. Increase heat; continue to stir. Remove from heat as it starts to boil.
Garnish with finely chopped onion greens.

More Recent Minnesotans

HISPANIC

Salsa

An all purpose favorite.
Ingredients:

4 large tomatoes, chopped (about 3 cups)
1/2 cup chopped green onions (white parts only)
1 small can (4 oz.) green chilis, chopped
2 tbsp. vinegar (red wine, preferably)
1-1/2 tbsp. sugar
1/2 tsp. salt
1/4 tsp. hot sauce (or more to taste)
Combine all ingredients: refrigerate at least 4 hours before serving.

Guacamole

Serve with hot chips as an hors d'oeuvres or as a side dish.
Ingredients for dip to serve 10:

4 avocados (or 3 large)
3 tbsp. lemon juice, fresh
1/3 cup finely chopped scallions
1/3 cup finely chopped coriander
salt to taste

Cut each avocado in two: scoop flesh into a bowl. Mash with a fork.
Add other ingredients, stir thoroughly and salt to taste.
Serve with hot tortilla chips.

Tamales

tamale dough

Ingredients:

3 cups corn tortilla flour
1 cup vegetable shortening (traditionally lard)
1 tsp. baking powder
1-1/2 cups chicken broth
1 tsp. salt

Mix together (electric mixer) the shortening, baking powder and salt
until light and creamy (about 3 minutes). Mix in the flour, a little at a
time.
Heat the broth (only until warm - not hot) and mix into the shortening-
flour.
(The traditional test to see if the mixture is sufficiently fluffy is to see if
a bit of it will float momentarily on the surface of cold water).

To make tamales

The tamales are wrapped in corn husks (some Central American
countries use banana leaves). Husks may be purchased in Mexican food
markets or you could save them after serving corn on the cob. Soak
the husks overnight, weighed down to submerge.
Fill one husk at a time. Lay the husk on a flat surface. Place 2 tbsps. of

dough in the center of each husk and spread it over a 3 inch square area. Place 1 tbsp. of filling (recipes follow) as a strip down the center of the square of dough. Pull the sides of the husk together, sealing the filling in the dough.

Roll the husk - loosely.

Tie the ends with a narrow strip of husk or fold the ends over.

Steam a stack of tamales in a steamer for about 1-1/2 hours.

filling recipe #1

Ingredients:

6 cups of bell pepper strips: use a variety of colors
1 cup of cheese of your choosing, grated
3 tbsp. vegetable oil

Sauté the pepper strips in the oil over medium heat until soft (10-15 minutes). Mix with grated cheese.

filling recipe #2

Ingredients:

1 pound pork, cut into strips
1 tsp. minced garlic
1 cup hot enchilada sauce

Let the pork marinate 1 hour in the sauce and garlic, refrigerated.

Chicken Chili over Rice

This one's pretty hot; check it out as you go.
Ingredients for 6 servings:

2 pounds skinned boneless chicken, cut into strips
1 tbsp. olive oil
2 onions, chopped fine
2 tbsp. minced garlic
2 - 16 oz. cans kidney or chili beans
1-1/2 cup chicken stock
3 medium Jalapeno peppers, seeded and chopped*

1 tsp. Tabasco sauce
3 tbsp. powdered cumin
2 tbsp. dried oregano

Sauté onion and garlic in oil until onion is translucent; do not burn. Add chicken, cumin and oregano to skillet. Sauté 3 minutes, stirring continuously. Add all other ingredients. Continue to cook over medium heat until chicken is tender (about 10 minutes).
Serve over rice.

Possible toppings (pass in separate bowls):

1 green (bell) pepper, seeded, diced or cut into strips
6 scallions, sliced
6 tbsp. shredded cheese (Monterey Jack works well)

use kitchen gloves when handling hot peppers

Stuffed Bell Peppers

Ingredients to serve 6:

6 large bell peppers
1 pound ground beef
1 onion, chopped
1 tbsp. minced garlic
1/2 cup fresh coriander, chopped
1 tsp. Worcestershire sauce
Tabasco sauce to taste
3 tbsp. vegetable oil
2 eggs

Coat peppers with oil; place balance of oil in a skillet. Fry until skin begins to curl. Let cool. Peel and remove seeds.
Using same oil, crumble ground beef and fry until brown. At the same time (with the hamburger), fry the onions, garlic and coriander. Mix in Worcestershire and Tabasco sauces.
Stuff peppers.
Beat the eggs. Dip the peppers in the egg and fry in oil - all sides.

Egg Timbales

Ingredients to serve 6:

4 eggs
1 tbsp. butter
1 small can (4 oz.) mild green chilis
1 cup light cream
1/4 tsp. pepper, freshly ground
1/8 t Tabasco sauce
1/3 cup fine bread crumbs
6 servings, sliced, pre-cooked ham
1 small jar (2 oz.) pimentos

Rub the insides of custard cups with butter. Coat insides of cups with bread crumbs. Beat eggs. Add and mix together chilis, cream, pepper and Tabasco sauce. Pour into cups.
Bake in a medium oven for about 30 minutes or until a knife comes out clean.
Place a serving of heated ham on each plate. Turn cups upside down. By sliding a table knife along the inside of each cup the timbales will drop out onto the ham.
Garnish with pimentos.

Asian

Rice Cakes

Ingredients for 4 servings:

1 cup cooked rice
7/8 cup flour
1 cup milk
3 eggs
dash of salt
1 tsp. baking powder
2 tbsp. sugar

Combine the milk and the egg yolks and beat until it starts to get "frothy".
Combine and thoroughly mix sugar, flour, baking powder and salt.

Beat the egg whites until they "peak' easily.

Combine and thoroughly mix together all ingredients. Fry (like pancakes) on a hot griddle.

Fried Rice

Ingredients to serve 4:

4 cups cooked rice
1 onion, chopped
3 tbsp. vegetable oil
2 eggs
1/2 cup chopped mushrooms
1/2 cup chopped ham (or other cooked meat)
2 tbsp. soy sauce
salt and pepper to taste

Pre-cook the rice.

Sauté the chopped onion in the oil. Add the chopped mushrooms the last minute or so.

Add the rice and continue to sauté for 2 minutes.

Beat the chopped meat and soy sauce into the eggs and add to the pan. Stir together thoroughly. Continue to heat for about 5 minutes or until eggs are no longer runny; stirring regularly.

Eggplant with Pork

Ingredients to serve 8:

2 large eggplants
1/2 pound pork roast or other tender cut
2 tbsp. soy sauce

Cut the pork into narrow strips. Place in a saucepan and cover with water. Add soy sauce. Heat to boiling then reduce heat to simmer. Cook, uncovered, until tender.

Cut each eggplant into four servings: leave skin on. Cook until tender. Serve egg plants with pork slivers.

Chicken with Egg Crust

Ingredients to serve 4:

1 chicken
3 tbsp. soy sauce
1/2 pound fresh mushrooms, sliced
3 tbsp. cooking oil
1 pkg. frozen peas
4 tbsp. sugar
1 medium onion, sliced and broken into rings
dash of salt
2 tbsp. sake
3 eggs

Cut the chicken meat from the bones and slice into bite-size pieces.
Place chicken pieces in a saucepan. Cover with water. Add soy sauce.
Bring to a boil, reduce heat and cook until tender (not over-done).
Meanwhile, sauté sliced onion and mushrooms in the oil until onion is
translucent. In a separate pan, cover the peas with water, add the sugar
and a dash of salt. Bring to a boil, reduce heat and cook until tender.
Remove the cooked chicken from its saucepan and add to the pan
containing the peas. Add the onion and mushrooms. Add the sake.
Combine the 3 eggs and beat until well mixed (uniform color). Pour the
eggs over the contents of the saucepan. Cook until the eggs form a
crust. Cut egg crusts into 4 pieces. Remove contents with a slotted
spoon (egg on top). Pour a little of the liquid over each serving.

Spicy Shrimp with Tomato Sauce

Ingredients for 6 servings:

2-1/2 pounds of shrimp that have been peeled and deveined
1 large egg
3 tbsp. vegetable oil
3 tbsp. catsup
7 tbsp. cornstarch
water to dissolve cornstarch
1 tbsp. fish stock (if available)
1/2 cup rice wine (or cooking sherry)
2 tbsp. chopped green onions (including greens)
1 tbsp. sugar

1 tbsp. ginger root, grated
1 tbsp. garlic, minced
1 tbsp. vinegar (preferably rice)

Beat egg into 1 cup of water. Dip shrimp into egg wash and then into cornstarch. Stir fry in hot wok 2 or 3 minutes.

Add fish stock (or 1 tbsp. water) and catsup, cook a few seconds, and then add all remaining ingredients, stir fry for another 2 minutes. (longer if shrimp are not white).

Poached Duck

Ingredients to serve 4:

1 large, domestic duck or 2 wild ducks
6 ribs celery, cut into chunks
1 large onion, sliced and broken into rings
1 orange - peelings only
6 tbsp. soy sauce
1/2 tsp. salt

Clean duck thoroughly inside and out. Remove any pinfeathers.
Place duck (or ducks, if small) in a kettle. Cover with water. Add all other ingredients. Bring water to a boil, then reduce heat to simmer. Cook until tender (about 3 hours).

Sweet and Sour Pork

Ingredients for 6 servings:

2 pounds lean pork (tender cut) cut into 1-1/2 inch by 1/2 inch pieces
1 cup flour
1 large onion, broken into rings
1 large green (bell) pepper, seeded and sliced
1 tsp. ginger, minced
1 cup small, sweet peas
2 carrots, sliced or cut into strips
4 tbsp. vegetable oil
salt and pepper to season pork

Using 2 tbsp. oil, dredge the pork strips in flour and sauté, turning strips occasionally. Be sure the pork is done but not over-done.

Using 2 tbsp. oil, sauté the onion and pepper, add the ginger (use a heavy skillet or wok).

Meanwhile, cook the carrots and peas in boiling water until tender.

Fish and Eggs

Ingredients for 4:

2 de-boned fillets from a two to three pound white-meated fish (about 3/4 pounds of meat)
8 eggs
1 tsp. salt
3 tbsp. sake
3 tbsp. soy sauce
4 tbsp. sugar
6 tbsp. water
vegetable oil for frying

Grind the fish fillets or chop fine. Mix the salt and sugar with the fish - evenly.

Break the eggs into a mixing bowl. Add the sake, soy sauce, and water. Beat until a uniform yellow color.

Add the ground (or chopped) fish to the bowl. Stir together thoroughly.

Using a pan* (traditional) or a griddle, pour mixture forming 4 individual patties of equal size. Brown on both sides, using a spatula to turn (very carefully so that it does not break apart.

Remove from pan or griddle and place on waxed paper. Roll up each patty and secure with toothpicks. Cut into slices about 3/4 inch wide.

*traditionally, 7 inch square pans are used, making square patties.

Sweet Rice Pudding

May be used as a dessert or as a side dish.
Ingredients for 6 servings:

2-1/2 cups rice
2-1/2 cups water, divided
15 dates, pitted and chopped
1 cup lotus seeds, pre-cooked (if unavailable, use other seeds, such as caraway or sunflower)

1/2 cup dried and chopped apricots
3 tbsp. raisins
1 cup red bean paste (optional)
8 tbsp. sugar
2 tbsp. vegetable oil
1 tbsp. cornstarch, diluted in 1 tbsp. water

Soak rice in cold water 2 hours; drain.

Steam rice (45 minutes). Stir in 1 cup water, vegetable oil and one-half of the sugar.

Place the fruit and lotus seeds over the bottom of a large bowl that can be used for steaming. Cover fruit with half the rice. Cover with red bean paste. Add the balance of the rice. Steam for 30 minutes.

Meanwhile, prepare a sauce of 1 cup of water and the remaining sugar. Bring to a boil, reduce heat and then add the cornstarch mixed with water to thicken.

Place the rice-fruit mixture on salad plates and then sprinkle sauce over each helping.

India

Roast Leg of Lamb

Although major Indian cultures do not eat meat, others do. You may also want to try these seasonings with beef or pork.

Ingredients to serve 6:

5 or 6 pound leg of lamb (fat removed)
2 tsp. curry powder
1 onion, chopped
1/4 tsp. cayenne pepper
1 tbsp. grated ginger root
1/2 tsp. salt
1 tsp. pepper
1 tbsp. minced garlic
3 tbsp. lemon juice
1 tbsp. Dijon mustard

Combine all seasoning ingredients in a blender until smooth.

Make a dozen one inch slits in the leg. Work the seasonings into these cuts.

Place the leg on a rack in a roasting pan. Roast in a 350° oven for about 2 hours or until desired doneness is achieved. If you have a meat thermometer, insert it into the heavier part of the leg - but not touching bone. Lamb will be rare at 140° and well done at 170°.

Lentils and Curried Rice

Serve as a side dish.
Ingredients to serve 4:

1 cup lentils
1 cup long grain rice
1 large onion, broken into circles
2 cups water
2 tsp. curry powder
4 tsp. chopped parsley
vegetable oil

Cook the lentils in the water until tender (about 15 minutes).
Meanwhile, sauté the onion rings in oil until translucent.
Cook rice in 2 tbsp. oil until done; stirring continuously.
Toss lentils, onions and rice with seasonings.

Curried Vegetables

Serve as a side dish:
Ingredients to serve 6:

2 cups cauliflower, cut bite-size
2 cups broccoli, cut bite-size
1 cup peas
6 small potatoes (new, if available)
1 onion, chopped
3 tbsp. vegetable oil
2 cups water
1 tbsp. curry powder
1 tsp. salt
1 tsp. cumin, ground
1 tsp. coriander, ground

In an iron kettle, brown the potatoes in oil. Add onion, cook until translucent. Add water and all seasonings. Bring to a boil and then reduce heat and simmer 10 minutes. Add remaining vegetables and continue to cook until done but crisp.

Remove vegetables from water with a slotted spoon.

Curry Paste for Seasoning

Ingredients for about 1/2 cup:

8 peppercorns
1 tsp. mustard seeds
1/4 tsp. coriander seeds
1 tsp. cumin seeds
2 tbsp. chopped onion
2 cloves garlic
2 tbsp. ginger root, grated or chopped fine
1 inch lemon grass (lower part of stalk)
1 tsp. turmeric

Into a pre-heated, dry skillet, drop the peppercorns, mustard seeds, coriander seeds and cumin seeds. Stir as they heat. Cover when seeds start to pop. Shake the skillet as you continue to cook for about 2 minutes (do not burn).

Grind the toasted seeds into a powder.

Into a running food processor, place the garlic, onion, ginger root and lemon grass. When well blended, add the powdered spices and the turmeric. Blend a little further until it has a pasty consistency. Paste may be stored, refrigerated, up to one week.